Advance Praise for *Luck by Design*

"*Luck by Design* provides solid guidance to help you *wonder about* your life instead of merely *wandering through* it. Goldman shares a lot of practical insights from his successful business career. These can make a difference in yours."

—Roger von Oech, author,
A Whack on the Side of the Head

"In today's world, college students and recent grads face new challenges, every day. *Luck by Design* shows that attaining success is a choice that you have, every day, in school and in the world. And the sooner you get started, the sooner you move in that direction, the better."

—Richard L. McCormick, President,
Rutgers University, New Brunswick, NJ

"Unlike many other successful entrepreneurs, Goldman didn't stop pushing himself after making a lot of money. Instead, he grappled with some of life's Big Questions in pursuit of meaning. His story and insights are inspiring: it *is* possible to win big in business with heart as well as mind."

—Ben Casnocha, author,
My Start-Up Life: What a (Very) Young CEO Learned on His Journey Through Silicon Valley

"In *Luck by Design*, Richie Goldman, a successful, self-made entrepreneur, makes a convincing and engaging argument for his deeply-held belief that life's solutions are in your hands. No matter where you are now, the potential for change, growth and learning is yours."

—Janet L. Holmgren, President,
Mills College, Oakland, CA

"There are two kinds of luck: the luck that we go out and find, and the luck that we hope finds us. We can trust the first with our lives; the second will always let us down. Richie Goldman's heartfelt book tells us exactly how to create the first, enriching our personal, business, and inner lives every step of the way. For anyone about to embark on the adventure of life, *Luck by Design* will be a warm and supportive friend."

—Dan Roam, author,
The Back of the Napkin: Solving Problems and Selling Ideas With Pictures

"This is a great time to be young or climbing a career ladder –if you listen to Richie Goldman. He challenges us to go beyond job titles to craft a life that anticipates an uncertain economic future. Combining practical advice with hard-won wisdom from the world of corporate America, Goldman will convince you to create your own *Luck by Design* by embarking on a difficult, courageous and ultimately rewarding journey."

—BRUCE R. MAGID, DEAN,
BRANDEIS INTERNATIONAL BUSINESS SCHOOL, WALTHAM, MA

"Richie Goldman speaks the truth about how to find the kind of success we are all seeking. He speaks with authority and authenticity. Take it from him; he knows what he is talking about!"

—RABBI SHERRE HIRSCH, AUTHOR,
*WE PLAN, GOD LAUGHS: TEN STEPS TO FINDING YOUR DIVINE PATH
WHEN LIFE IS NOT TURNING OUT LIKE YOU WANTED*

Luck by Design

Certain Success in an Uncertain World

RICHARD E. GOLDMAN

MORGAN JAMES PUBLISHING • NEW YORK

Published by:
Morgan James Publishing, LLC
1225 Franklin Ave Ste 32
Garden City, NY 11530-1693
Toll Free 800-485-4943

ISBN: 978-1-60037-433-3 (Paperback)
       978-1-60037-432-6 (Hardcover)

Library of Congress Control Number: 2008936943

Epigraph from *Half Asleep in Frog Pajamas* by Tom Robbins, copyright © 1994 by Tom Robbins. Used by permission of Bantam Books, a division of Random House, Inc.

Dedicated
with love
to
the Goldman girls
Ava and Zaia
and
the Goldman women
Beeb, Ethel, Weez, Traci, and Emily

He's not really a fighter. He's an adventurer. There's a difference. He doesn't attack, he engages; he doesn't defend, he expands; he doesn't destroy, he transforms; he doesn't reject, he explores…

TOM ROBBINS, *HALF ASLEEP IN FROG PAJAMAS*

Contents

RICHARD E. GOLDMAN

To the Children of the Baby Boom Generation:

On behalf of my entire generation, I apologize. We — the great Baby Boom generation, we who were going to change the world — certainly have. Except we haven't exactly changed it for the better. We missed a few steps along the way. If you feel disenfranchised or alienated, you are not alone. Despite our good intentions, the Baby Boomers have compromised your future.

A few examples:

• We have altered the notion of "family" by divorcing in more than one of every two marriages, often leaving you on unmanageable and unstable ground.

• We have run up tremendous personal debt, living a lifestyle generally beyond our means, forcing you to run up your own debt just trying to go to college and to live day to day.

• Our federal government, which helped *our* parents buy homes, build cities, and educate their children is now swimming in debt.

• We have found no solution to our nearly cracking Social Security system.

• We have made incremental progress, but not solved the problems of world hunger, poverty, HIV, AIDS, or any of a multitude of other diseases.

• We have continued to pollute the environment, to the point that before long there might not be an environment as we now know it. This alone may render meaningless all of our other mistakes.

• We, who were dealt perhaps the best hand ever and who have been witness to many of the most powerful and inspiring people in history, can only hope that great people remain for you to emulate.

• We have tarnished the global image of our country in ways that might prove difficult to correct.

• And finally… we've left you with one nation — undereducated.

Our bad.

But there *are* solutions, all of which require hard work, careful thought, consistent effort — and the luck that *you* can create to help in all you do, every day.

Richie

Preface

You MIGHT HAVE HEARD THAT now is a terrible time to be young. Certainly the Open Letter you've just read would make it seem so. But guess what? If it is *now* and if you are *young*, you have no choice. You didn't choose this time to be young; it chose you. This is a terrific example of one of the primary tenets of life: you choose some things, and some things choose you. It's what *you* choose and the process that *you* use in making those choices that determine the course and character of your life. *Luck by Design* will help you to make better, more informed, and wiser decisions about the things that you choose. It will help you to be better at handling, acknowledging, and embracing those things that choose you. It will help you know, understand, and deal with the facts and challenges that you will face. It will also help you to live a happy, prosperous, and fulfilling life—however many years of it you have ahead of you. No doubt about it: that's a lot to ask of one book.

Chances are you've read a self-help book or two. In most of them, the author makes a basic assumption—you are broken. Therefore, all you need to do is read the book, follow the steps, and you will be fixed. This book challenges that assumption with the following simple truth: your life is not a problem to be solved. Instead, it is a miracle of an opportunity to experience all the unexplored aspects of your being. This book will show you that the solutions are in your hands and they are in your hands *now*. And more: the solutions have been in your hands since you became a conscious being. *Luck by Design* will help you to access your own capabilities and competency, not by rote "how-tos" but by digging in to find your authentic self. What it requires of you is deep and personal honesty, courage, commitment, and fortitude. Easier said than done? Yes and no. Yes, because if you could do it, you already would be. And no, because the focus and control over your life is not something to be found on the outside; it's all on the inside. Like anything else you'll encounter in your life, the potential for change, growth, and learning is in your hands—and another choice that *you have*. If you don't like what's happening in your outer life experience, then *now* is the time to review, revise, and reclaim your right heading.

Who Should Read This Book?

In my work at Men's Wearhouse over three decades, in my family life, and in my volunteer activities, I have seen that the children of Baby Boomers have a perspective and world experience that is vastly different than that of their parents. In writing this book, I have had the children of Boomers in mind as the primary audience. So if you are starting college, in college, beginning your working life, or climbing up the ladder of your career, as you read *Luck by Design*, you will find practical solutions to everyday situations and problems.

You'll find advice that comes from my experiences managing people in your parents' generation of workers and in your own. You'll find work advice and life advice that will help to draw luck toward you. It's not an Easy button, but a way of life that can be ever improving.

Who Am I, and Why Did I Write This?

My formative years were about as far removed from today's digital age as could be while still living in the United States. I grew up in a middle-class Jewish family in Hazleton, Pennsylvania, a small coal-mining town in decline as the coal industry was sliding out of favor nationally. My father owned and ran a local retail store, Boston Hardware, as had his father before him. It was a family enterprise, and all of us, including my siblings and our mother and aunt, helped out.

I was not a great student. In fact, I was a rather poor student at the private high school I attended in Freeland, an even smaller coal-mining town ten miles from Hazleton. A wealthy coal-mining family had founded the school, Mining and Mechanical Institute (MMI), to educate the miners and their sons. MMI's motto was, "Making men individuals." It was certainly the case for me, although I doubt that I was the kind of "individual" that MMI had in mind. At MMI, I discovered that I had an eye for the arts but was overwhelmed by a math- and science-dominated environment in which, no matter how hard I tried, I failed (or came very close to it). I had an ear for dissent, which I was always ready, willing, and able to try. I also had a mouth for trouble, which I was constantly in. My behavior was a simple response to the complicated issue of barely surviving academically and feeling like I was not living up to the expectations of others (the school and members of my extended family), despite my best efforts.

Thankfully, survival turned into success. In September 1968, I enrolled at Rutgers University in New Brunswick, New Jersey— my father's alma mater. It was the beginning of an experience as completely positive as high school had been utterly negative. It was both the time (1968–72) and the place (a very liberal university) that piqued my interest, enthusiasm, and creativity. My formal education and the many things I learned outside the classroom opened up avenues for exploration that I continued to follow for the rest of my life. Rutgers helped to show me my potential, instead of belaboring my weaknesses. Positive as the experience was, I didn't acquire any academic honors, other than a BA in English and a great interest in (and little practical knowledge of) advertising.

My degree in hand, I returned to Hazleton to work at my father's store. It had never been explicitly stated, but for some time I had thought that it was going to be my destiny to take over the store one day. After about a year, however, I realized that this was *not* what I wanted to do for the rest of my life. Although my father was a patient and understanding teacher, I was a restless kid who just couldn't adjust to small-town life after my college experience. I had an incredible urge to go out into the world and make my own mark. Buoyed with my BA in English and an independent study paper written while at Rutgers, titled "The Psychology of Television Advertising," I was confident that Houston advertising agencies would be clamoring for my talents. So in 1973, I moved from Hazleton to Houston, Texas, with all of my worldly possessions in the trunk of my car and about $300 in my pocket. It was a bold and impetuous move, which somehow I did with a lot of confidence.

At age twenty-two, I had decided that I was willing and able to live my dream—or at least what I *thought* at the time was my dream. I struggled a bit, made a few false starts, and soon found a closely related dream that set me on a career path for the next twenty-nine years of my life. It was a path that enabled me to retire long before standard retirement age—and without any financial worries. By moving to Houston when I did, I put myself in the right place at the right time. My decision to move and then *acting* on that decision came from a place of deep personal trust. Although I could then barely fathom this place, and certainly could not verbalize it, what I did was act upon that trust rather than think about it, procrastinate, or second-guess myself. I was in touch with my higher self, mostly because I was very young and very open.

Did I realize all of this at the time? Of course not—and that's not the point. The point is that I knew that *something* was going on, and my inner voice told me to pay attention. And most important, I listened. Doing that allowed me to rewrite the rules that had been placed on me by others up until then. I allowed myself to be open to what I wanted, and I began to write my own rules. These rules and some of the stories of my life are laced throughout the book, told not for the sake of my story but to help *you* develop your own.

I've often been told how "lucky" I have been in my career. For a long time I questioned the idea myself. However, one day I finally realized that it wasn't luck at all. I made one thing happen (moving to Houston), which, after a few more steps, landed me at the door of Men's Wearhouse back when it was just one store with a hand-lettered sign. I was with Men's Wearhouse as it rose from obscurity to a nationally known business. Dumb luck? More like some luck! Or, as the innovative Major League Baseball executive Branch Rickey once said, "Luck is the residue of design."

In this book, I share with you some of my own design in hopes of helping you create your own luck. You want to win the lottery? Go ahead, buy your tickets. It's a great fantasy—but little more than that. *Luck by Design* puts wheels under your wagon and enables you to be off to your destined adventure. This book is all about helping you learn how to create your own luck, by design.

What's Here, and How Can You Use It?

Now that you've got some background on the purpose of the book and on me, how can you use it? First is the obvious: read. As the American writer Samuel Clemens (better known by his pseudonym, Mark Twain) has been quoted, "The man who does not read . . . has no advantage over the man who cannot read." Understand that holding the book in your hands will not increase your luck. Flipping the pages will not increase your luck. It's reading the book and putting it to use that will help you design luck for your life. Many of the ideas here I've run past a wide-ranging group of people I like to call my advisory board. These are people whose ages range from seventeen to forty, with circumstances and questions that may be very similar to yours. Over the course of the book, you'll learn more about how they enlightened me.

Now that you've nearly read the preface, ahead are nine chapters, a postscript, and a reference list. But first, here are a handful of tips before you read on:

1. Take your time. Reading the book is not a race. Reading it and using it well is a process.

2. As you read, you'll find a number of places in which you're told to **stop!** This is not a test; there's no one standing nearby to demand that you shut the book. It's just that you'll get more from your reading if you actually take the time to stop and actively consider the questions raised.

3. Each chapter has at least a reminder or two in the margins. These exist to reinforce important points, in case you miss the overarching one, which is to be present while you read and to attend to what you read as you read it—just as you attend to your life as it unfolds.

4. I've had successes and made my share of mistakes over the years. Some of these are encapsulated in the "Lesson Learned" sections that conclude each of the chapters, starting with chapter 2. Reading them may just keep you from repeating some of my mistakes.

5. I'll also be supplementing *Luck by Design* through my website, www.richiegoldman.com, which will include a Q&A section, a reading list with books that should be useful to you on your journey, and further tips. There you

will also have the opportunity to share your design with me and with the other readers of this book.

How you use the lessons in *Luck by Design* is up to you. My advice? Keep an open heart and an open mind. Read on. Enjoy the process.

1

It's In Your Hands

Yes, you have inherited the "perfect storm" of problems at the national and global levels. Much of it may be on my shoulders, together with those of the other Baby Boomers, but the reality is that many of the solutions are in your hands. And you have the time ahead of you that Boomers do not. Along with this responsibility, you have your personal life challenges. You might view the world with great pessimism. You have been told that you are the first generation to predict that your life prospects will be less than those of your parents in terms of opportunities for advancement and financial rewards. You live in a world where change occurs in seconds, not days or weeks. Your competition in the job world is not simply local or national, but global. It might seem like everywhere you look there are threats—to your economic future, to your political freedoms, to the environment, and to your own safety.

And everywhere you look, there are great opportunities as well. Is it possible that your life will be far *more* productive, fulfilling, and engaged than the lives of those in your parents' generation? Is it possible that rapid change is an asset, not a liability? And is it possible that although the competition is global, the opportunities are global as well? And is it possible that the threats can be windows of opportunity for social and global change? The answer to all of the above is an emphatic *yes*!

The Basics

As a foundation for moving forward, think of the following as "givens," even though for now you might not believe or fully understand them. More information will come later, in this book and in your life, to help explain. In the meantime, know this:

- Life is not hard. It is complex, and it is unpredictable, but it's not hard. You want to know hard? How about a world without antibiotics or polio vaccinations? How about the homeless in our country, or the starving people in Somalia? How about the Great Depression?

- Life is a series of illusions and disillusions. You move from the comfort of the womb and the comfort of the breast to the harsh reality that we're all flawed human beings and that somehow, despite our flaws, all of our lives are enhanced when we work together.

- You are not broken. You are a piece of unformed clay, and you are the artist whose duty is to create the magnificent being that you truly can be.

- The more gracefully you can accept how things are at the moment—not how your desires and preferences want them to be—the more energy and joy you will experience.

- Whatever you really want, you already have all the inner resources you need to make it happen. You need to learn to trust that you are in the right place at the right time to allow yourself to learn and to make something happen for yourself.

- Everything in your external world comes to you as a lesson; if you pay attention and stay awake, you will learn quickly. Every lesson—good or bad—is a great gift. Take it as such. You can figure it all out *for* yourself, and you don't have to figure it all out *by* yourself.

- You are powerful. Surprised? Even if you haven't thought of yourself as powerful, you've been so since you were about two years old. Why do you think they call it the "terrible twos"? Because it was all about your unstructured yet powerful realization that there was power in the word *no* and that by using no (albeit over and over again), you could get attention. Your power is still there; it's just been diminished a bit by time and your own life experiences.

- Learn it now, or learn it later: there are certain immutable laws. Among them are that you are going to have the following in your lifetime: pain, loss, suffering, gain, and success. How you respond to these is what defines who you are and the course of your life. (Hint: you respond to all of them in the same way … with equanimity, grace,

3

humility, reverence, and thanks.) This book will help you access your own ability to handle whatever life hands you and to grow a big enough personal container so that none of what life doles out will knock you off balance.

- You have a place on this earth, and you have a reason for being. Your job, obligation, and sacred contract is to figure it out. At the most global level, you are here to leave the world a better place than it was when you got here.

- Heroes are a dime a dozen. *Real* heroes are few and far between. This book will help you emulate the real heroes of the world. It will help you to become that which you emulate in others. You can be the real hero of your own life and the lives of others.

- Life is a process, not a destination. Everyone starts out at the beginning, bagging groceries, as it were. From this point forward, instead of looking at the end result—the success of a person, the success of a team, a beautiful painting—think about the time, effort, and love that went into making it happen. Learn to accept life on its own terms. Take the journey. It's called a *process*.

- You will hear *no* far more often than you will hear *yes*. Accept this and move on. Use no as a test of your inner desire to get something accomplished. Understand that *no* is an outer reflection, usually from someone else; your own heart and your own gut are the inner reflection.

- Life is not going to hand you what you want; you're going to have to create it. Life *will* give you the chance to "get it." Use this book as part of the toolkit for your creation.

The Journey Ahead

This can be the beginning of a life-changing journey for you. It can be a journey of self-discovery and a journey that opens your eyes to your own possibilities. It can also be the journey that sets you on the path of finding your place in this world and your true calling. Or it can be a waste of your time. The book is in your hands, and the work is up to *you*. Will you choose to do the work? You're going on the journey anyway; consider the upside of doing the work.

HOW CAN MY JOURNEY HELP YOU ON YOURS?

Sandwiched between my older sister, a whiz-bang student and ace Girl Scout, and my precocious younger brother, who was the talk of the town, or at least the talk of the neighborhood, I was neither a great student nor particularly outspoken. It was only natural, then, that I was constantly being compared to both my sister and brother. And it was likewise natural for me, the quiet one, to take this comparison very personally. While I am no therapist, I do know (now) that this truth was a gift that opened up countless paths in a life of self-reflection.

If you've read the preface, you know already that I was never the perfect student. While my grades were As and Bs in grade school and middle school, my teachers constantly told me that I could do better and asked why I didn't perform as well as my siblings. I didn't know what doing "better" meant, especially in light of my grades, and I couldn't comprehend the comparisons. With no understanding of how to process the criticism, I began to believe it, to take it to heart, and to doubt my own abilities and question my self-worth. By the eighth grade, even though I was still in search of "better," I began to flounder. By my senior year of high school, I had all but given up. Still, I slogged along, requesting a transfer into the section that was not "advanced" but "less than advanced." My grades were awful, my attitude worse. Graduation was a relief, and to this day, I'm proud to say that I graduated eighteenth in my class. And unless I revealed it, who would guess that the class consisted of only twenty-six students?

The leap from a small school in a coal-mining community to Rutgers University in New Brunswick, New Jersey, was a big one. Although the prospect of being a classic small-town boy thrown into the big-school environment was terrifying, I realized that this was a chance to reinvent myself, to respond creatively and with a renewed sense of enthusiasm for dealing with life's challenges. I thrived at Rutgers and succeeded in reinventing myself, so it should not have been a surprise that I didn't last in Hazleton long after graduation. Thanks to my college experiences, I once again trusted life at this point. My decisions were part of my own master plan.

Trust life. Make decisions as part of your own master plan.

After arriving in Houston, I went out to get the advertising job of my dreams. My first agency interview was most promising. I had found Marcom-Day Advertising in the Yellow Pages. It was a meager shop, just down the street from my more meager apartment. It had five employees and a handful of clients.

How did I get the interview? In retrospect, it must have been because Bob Day, the owner, couldn't believe my chutzpah. Who was this kid who just walked in the door late on a Friday afternoon and asked for an interview, with nothing: no appointment, no resume, and no portfolio—nada. What I lacked in brains and experience, I made up for in guts and enthusiasm. I wanted to work at an advertising agency; of that, I was certain. When Bob resisted hiring me by telling me that there wasn't enough business at the agency to warrant another salary, I countered by telling him I'd bring business to the agency. No doubt startled at the thought, if not intrigued by the prospect, Bob told me that if I could bring enough business to the agency, the next time they needed to hire someone, it would be me. Bob and I shook hands on the deal, and I was out of there. I didn't have a job, but that didn't faze me; I had a *prospective* job. I went home and spent the weekend mentally turning down fantastic offers from countless other advertising agencies.

But it wasn't that simple. Unfortunately, my interview with Bob was not only the first, but it was also the best. Other agencies that I approached were clearly not interested in my talents and I was turned down coldly, most often rudely. On the few occasions when I did get past the receptionist, my obvious lack of experience was soon unearthed, and my plea for a job was turned down. Yet I didn't let it demoralize me and I kept on plowing ahead. I knew, deep down inside, that everything was going to work out.

After three stinging weeks of rejection and of sweltering as I drove around in my un-air-conditioned car in the ninety-degree Houston heat, I ran out of money, ran out of guts, and had to look for a real job. Although I believed that advertising was still my calling, Bob Day was not calling. I needed a job—any job. The calling would have to wait.

I found a job selling display-advertising space in an all-advertising, free weekly circular called the *Greensheet*. The paper consisted mostly of classified ads—people selling everything from new kittens to used cars. The rest of the paper was display advertising, placed mostly by retail stores. I had the perfect setup. I spent mornings on the phone, making calls to current customers; in the afternoons, I scoured the streets looking for new *Greensheet* customers—as well as looking for clients for Marcom-Day. I figured that any company that was inexperienced enough to buy an ad in the *Greensheet* would also need the expertise of an advertising agency like Marcom-Day.

A few weeks later, as I was driving around town making cold calls for the *Greensheet*, I drove by a shopping center consisting of a handful of retail stores and a dilapidated, yet well-known, steak house. In the middle of the shopping center sat a store with a crude, hand-painted, black-and-white wooden sign precariously attached to the roof of the building. The sign read, "The Men's Wearhouse." To me, it looked like an interesting prospect. I walked in, discussed the *Greensheet* with Harry Levy, one of George Zimmer's original partners, and sold him a quarter-page ad. A few days later, I returned with a sample of the ad and met George.

At that moment, did I know that Men's Wearhouse would eventually become a household name and a billion-dollar company with stores throughout the country? Did I know that I would play a big part in all of that? Did I know that I'd be inspired by and grow with my many co-workers? No, no, and no. But, even at that very young age, I did have a certain sense of where and how things should be for my life. By rewriting the rules for how my life should have been, I allowed myself to be open to what I *wanted*. And I had the sense to follow my intuition and see where my instincts and business sense would take me. But the happily-ever-after story most assuredly does *not* begin here. I took a few detours and stubbed my toes along the way.

I continued to sell ads for the *Greensheet*, while trying to lure customers to Marcom-Day Advertising and dreaming of working there.

> *Allow yourself to be open to what you want.*

And I stopped in at Men's Wearhouse every so often, because I had developed a friendship with both Harry and George. Despite having grown a clientele of small retailers who actually had wonderful success with their advertising (Men's Wearhouse was not one of them), I was becoming bored working at the *Greensheet*. At the same time, Men's Wearhouse had learned that advertising, including the *Greensheet* and most of their other advertising efforts, was not panning out. At my recommendation (and for a finder's fee of $600), Men's Wearhouse hired Marcom-Day Advertising. Marcom-Day immediately directed the media efforts for Men's Wearhouse to radio and newspaper only, eliminating everything else. That also meant they dropped the *Greensheet*. It was a small price for me to pay. And it also gave me a reason to occasionally go to Marcom-Day, to keep an eye on "my" account—Men's Wearhouse.

One day, while hanging out at Marcom-Day, I overheard a phone conversation between George and Drew Cherner, Marcom-Day's account executive for Men's Wearhouse. George was in search of a new employee and was offering $1,000 a month. As I sat there thinking about my current income of $800 a month, it dawned on me that *I* was the ideal candidate. I had retail experience from my father's store, and I had clothing experience from my days at Rutgers, where I sold shirts out of my fraternity house, and working one summer at Brotherhood, a retail-clothing store in State College, Pennsylvania. I expressed my interest to Drew, who suggested that I speak to George. I did, and the next thing I knew, I was in the retail business once again, working on the sales floor of Men's Wearhouse. It was October of 1973.

Marcom-Day's advertising efforts had begun to pay off, and Men's Wearhouse experienced a temporary lift in sales for the holiday season, but business slowed after the first of the year. I became bored again and anxious to get that advertising job. By comparison, standing on the floor of a retail store that wasn't doing a lot of business was backbreaking and mind numbing. By May of 1974, I knew I couldn't stay at Men's Wearhouse. It was then that I finally received the call I had been waiting for from Bob Day; he was ready to hire me. At that moment, there wasn't much to consider in making my decision to leave. My inner voice still wanted fame and fortune in the advertising business, and even though George and I had become good friends, I had this underlying advertising dream.

Before I left Men's Wearhouse to work at Marcom-Day, George made me an offer that he thought I couldn't refuse. He wanted me to buy stock in the company and be more than just a person on the sales floor—he wanted me to become his partner in the company. To his surprise, I turned him down. Again, I had this underlying advertising dream.

On my first day at Marcom-Day Advertising—in the very first minute that I sat in my new office—I knew I had made a giant mistake. My inner voice was screaming at me, but I didn't listen, believing that there was no way I could have made such a huge mistake. The screaming voice got hoarse, but that nagging feeling never left. Fortunately for me, six months later, George once more asked me to be his business partner, again offering stock, this time as an incentive to return. By this time, Men's Wearhouse had opened two more stores in Houston, so there was a lot more to do than be on the sales floor. Having by then realized that it was not so much a career in advertising that I wanted as a career advertising for Men's Wearhouse, I accepted his offer and returned to Men's Wearhouse for good in January of 1975.

George had originally hired me to work on the sales floor of the first (and only, at the time) Men's Wearhouse. I was not the executive vice president, and in fact, I was not any vice president at all. I was not the manager, or the assistant manager. I was a salesperson—a grocery bagger, if you will. I started at the very bottom. Upon my return to Men's Wearhouse, I took over responsibility for all aspects of advertising and began my work overseeing the merchandising for the company. My energy level ratcheted up a notch, and my new intent drew more opportunities to me. In retrospect, it was an example of intent magnetizing opportunities (the law of attraction at work). I bought the stock that

> *Intent magnetizes opportunities.*

George offered me, based on a decision I made and against outside advice, as you'll see in chapter 3. Twenty-nine years after I was first hired, I retired. Of course, a lot happened in those intervening years, much of which I've mined in writing this book.

11

Looking back, I realize that I expended very little energy worrying about my future as I was growing up. Others may have worried about me, but I recall thinking that I could do anything. The hitch was that I had no idea what "anything" was going to be. Well, here's a newsflash: I'm not that unique. You, too, can do anything. Your challenge, just as mine was, is to find out what that "anything" is; what's right for you. Much of this book is dedicated to helping you find the way to your own anything and helping you learn to paint the canvas of your own life. The big picture is this: somehow, some way, you need to find the ability to bridge your heart with your mind. To do so, you need to first *open* your heart and your mind.

In this book, I share with you many of the important lessons I learned while helping to create a company that went from obscurity to being a part of the national consciousness, at least in terms of men's apparel. I will share with you some of the great successes that the company had and that I had as well. And I'll share some of the failures. Failures? Why bother with failures? I look at failures because they are the ultimate opportunities in life. Failures are the benchmarks by which we can really define our souls and ourselves. They're often not pretty, but they're always important, and they're always defining—but only if you're paying attention and learning quickly.

Who Are You, and What About Your Journey?

What about your journey? Your journey is all about finding your sacred contract and your unique purpose in life. (There will be much more on that throughout the book.) You've made a good decision in buying *Luck by Design*. Doing so demonstrates a curiosity about looking into the unknown and expanding your own awareness. This book will help you to find your authentic self—someone who may not be the person you currently *think* you are. This person is the one who lies deep in your heart and your soul. It is the person who you *feel* you are and can be, and who is ready to come forward.

This book will help you to design your own empowerment—to learn and to understand that the life you've been given is one that you have great control over. This book is merely your toolbox for making all of this happen. The work is all up to you.

As you move on, ask yourself the following questions:

1. Do you have the courage to create your own destiny?
2. What would you choose to do in life, if whatever you chose as your goal were unequivocally guaranteed?
3. Can you build a big enough personal vessel to learn how to accept yourself for all of the good and all of the warts?
4. Can you learn how to accept and embrace change and realize that fluidity is part of a conscious and expanding mind?

Can you be an element of change? You can, and you *have to be.* As Gandhi said, "You must be the change you want to see in the world." In other words, you have to believe it and practice it before you can see it. Understand that your life is your message, and you write the rules.

Will you be able to turn around all of the woes that have been placed at your feet? Not by yourself. But one by one, you, along with the others who might read this book and the others with whom you interact, can begin to manifest change.

All of the problems mentioned in the Open Letter didn't happen overnight, nor did they happen as the result of the actions of one person. Many people were part of that process, and it is a process that can be changed and improved. It *has* to be. Once again, it's up to you.

You are about to find out what you can do, to find the width and depth of what you are capable of doing with your life. Love your life and use it well.

2

Life Is Misadvertised

LIFE AS IT APPEARS TO you from the media is not life as it really is. For example, consider advertising: the goal of any advertisement is to sell that particular product. Along with it, there's always another message. It's often disguised, but it's a message about you (as a member of the market the advertisers are attempting to reach). In the process of trying to sell toothpaste or deodorant, for example, advertisers also tell you the way that you "should" be.

And that's where the misadvertisement sneaks in. Over time, sometimes subtly, sometimes not, as we're constantly bombarded by ads depicting perfect people in perfect settings, we're led to believe that our lives are lacking. By comparison to the perfect people in the ads, we're not only lacking the product being advertised, but the benefit of the product as well; hence, we're lacking in general.

The same holds true for the other messages we get through media—the nonadvertising messages in the form of "news." Yet the media depicts only certain parts of life, and it is very selective in doing so. Media paints a certain "there" that exists in the world. It

15

creates the same landscape for millions of people who are nowhere near the same. But when you as an individual look at the media and then look at your own life, you find that they're very different—the "there" that is portrayed in the media is not the "here" that is you. Therefore, life is misadvertised.

So, it's misadvertised. What do I think accurate advertising for life would be? Would that opinion be relevant to you and to your life? Could there be accurate advertising for life? To know that, one would have to know the secrets to life, and there would have to be such a thing as completely accurate advertising—advertising that tells the whole truth and more and that doesn't play into contrived or real weaknesses. We know what life is not. Despite what the old song said, life is not a bowl of cherries. Nor is life like a box of chocolates, as Forrest Gump's mother advised him. Advertising is all about a vision for the future. And our view of life is wrapped up in our vision of the world and our place in it. What is the source of that vision? These are heady questions. But first we need to back up a bit.

Consider Your Vision

This chapter centers on the concept of vision, so a good place to start is to check out its definition. *Random House Webster's College Dictionary* defines vision as:

1. the act or power of sensing with the eyes; sight. 2. the act or power of anticipating that which will or may come to be; foresight: *entrepreneurial vision.*

"Sensing with the eyes" implies sensing with your own eyes, just as "foresight" implies your own foresight. "Vision" is clearly meant to be your own thing. Now think about this: what is your vision of the world? What is your vision of your place in the world? What is your vision of happiness? ***Stop!*** Close your eyes and think about any of these questions for a moment.

Chances are, the picture that you created in your mind's eye is not strictly your own vision. It's a vision based on information that you have gotten from the media. Whether through "unbiased" yet biased news stories, the subtle yet not-so-subtle advertising messages, or even that mass of information known as the Internet, what we learn from the outside world is all a vision—and all too often it's someone else's vision. Consequently, our behaviors, many of our opinions and values and what we each might see as our place in the world are also visions—again, quite possibly someone else's. As well, what we come to expect from the outside world is also a vision.

The influence of the media is all around, all the time; it influences all of us. But it is possible to become more savvy about the part that the media plays in your life and in the formulation of your opinions. The faulty assumptions you may make as a result of being influenced by media help to keep you from truly understanding your own self and your place in the world. By accepting the underlying reality of the title of this chapter, "Life Is Misadvertised," you can put yourself on the path of being a more critical thinker.

Saying that life is misadvertised assumes certain expectations. My expectations of life were very clearly formed by growing up in a particular time (the 50s and 60s) and place (Hazleton, Pennsylvania). It was an environment that influenced my personal sense of self and my sense of the rest of the world. Life for me in Hazleton was about as different as life can be imagined for a child growing up today, or for that matter, a child growing up ten or twenty years ago. Hazleton was a rural coal-mining town, secluded at the southern end of the Pocono Mountains. The nearest big cities were Philadelphia and New York City, more than one hundred miles away. Given the cars and roads of the day, that hundred-mile drive was vastly different than it is today.

The thirty thousand or so residents of Hazleton were an uncomfortable blend of Irish, Polish, Italian, and Jewish. For the most part, each group lived in their own section of town and generally had a mutual disdain for one another. There were no African Americans, no Hispanics, and no Asians. My "worldview" was about as far as I could see—pretty much to the end of my almost-all-Jewish block. Although we often went to New York City as children, the Big Apple was "there" as far as I was concerned. The world we saw there, while staying in Greenwich Village and going to Broadway shows, was only a small part of the big city, but it was enough to tell me that it was an entirely different world than ours.

My world—my "here"—was Hazleton. Any other "there," whether it was across the state, across the country, or across the world, was something I read about in books. My world was very insular, very controlled, and very safe. While the Cold War, Sputnik, and the Berlin Wall were all big world events, Hazleton seemed very far away from it all, and my place as a little boy in Hazleton made for an even deeper sense of remoteness. We played ball in the street, went in and out of each other's unlocked homes, and generally worried more about the Yankees than anything else.

With the exception of the Mickey Mouse Club, there was practically nothing on television that had any appeal to me or to my friends. Books were my main source of media entertainment. I went to the Hazleton Public Library weekly, borrowing the maximum four books at a time. The books I chose were always the same genre: two sports books, where the underdog somehow becomes the hero, and two books of history or biography about the early days of the United States.

Imagine it—limited television, no Internet, no voicemail, no email, no instant messaging, no Federal Express, no fax machines, no photocopiers, no computers, no calculators, and no Sesame Street. For that matter, no national fast food chains, like McDonalds, Pizza Hut, or KFC, and certainly no Starbucks. Compared to the early twenty-first century, I could have been living on a different planet. Come to think of it, in many ways, I was.

But even with my limited view of the world, my foundations and my visions of who I was and what my place was were formed from the outside, not the inside. At a very young age, I never imagined myself living anywhere else but Hazleton; I never imagined working anywhere but my father's store. My foundation came from what I knew. Beyond my forays to the library, what I knew of the world came mostly through the insular view of what came into Hazelton directly. Generations that followed built on a very different foundation.

What Is Your Source of Self?

Along with many of the Baby Boomers, I grew up as television was spreading geographically and its offerings and place in society were being forged. There were high hopes for what it would bring to all of us: education, community, and access to information. TV was a brand new and exciting medium—much as today's Internet in recent years. Before TV, newspapers and radio had been the primary source of information about the outside world. Television changed all of that, and for the first time in history, people across the United States became "connected" in a visual sense and almost in real time. It was revolutionary. Radio news broadcasts had been revolutionary in their time; TV expanded upon that revolution by adding film footage and the possibility of seeing events in real time, long distance. It was a far cry from news via radio, Teletype, or the pony express.

Technology has certainly advanced, and our sources for information have gone from the few to the infinite. In the process of writing this chapter, I've thought long and hard about the role of the Internet in everyday life. Certainly, everywhere you go, it's hard *not* to find someone using the Internet; there are few things more pervasive. It's a great place for information, but it has its drawbacks, as I'll articulate.

Years ago, an elderly Stanley Marcus (as in Neiman-Marcus) told me that the effect of the Internet on society was going to be equal to the invention of the wheel in its time. He was very right—but there is a big difference. I suppose that once everyone got the *idea* of the wheel, everyone could use it to their heart's content. There was little "controversy" as to its place in society, and there wasn't a lot of room for mistaking the wheel for something that it wasn't. That's not the case with the Internet.

The Internet is enabling us to be more aware and is giving us more opinions, but its vastness often creates more confusion than coherency. Even with the Internet, given today's supercharged political atmosphere and the global questions and problems that we face, there is little chance to get unbiased information. While the Internet might be boundless, it's also loaded with hyperbole masquerading as fact. If the lack of regulation on the Internet is its strongest asset, it is also its biggest weakness, as every day, tens of thousands of bogus news events are disseminated worldwide. Being "connected" also means that fact or fiction can make its way across the planet in a matter of minutes or hours, with not nearly enough fact checking to back it up. Long before the Internet, a popular saying had it that, "A lie can travel halfway around the world while the truth is putting on its shoes." Now, it could be that a lie can "travel *around* the world *twice* while the truth is *looking for* its shoes." Everything has sped up, even the speed with which news (whether truth, lies, or something in between) travels.

My bottom line about the Internet is the following: its role in being a major media player is indisputable, but it's still a work in progress and a work that will likely be dramatically changed in the next few decades. And anyone who tells you what the future of the Internet will be is a fool.

One doesn't have to go far to find advocates of the Internet in general, as well as the new and innovative changes that are taking place. Challenges are few and far between. But as you'll see throughout this book, I encourage you to challenge convention. I've done so myself and found a terrific, albeit controversial, book focused on the Internet and its potential downside: *The Cult of the Amateur: How*

Today's Internet Is Killing Our Culture by Andrew Keen. In perhaps the most compelling paragraph of the book, Keen argues:

> We—those of us who want to know more about the world, those of us who are the consumers of mainstream culture—are being seduced by the empty. promise of the "democratized" media. For the real consequence . . . is less culture, less reliable news, and a chaos of useless information. One chilling reality in this brave new digital epoch is the blurring, obfuscation, and even disappearance of truth. (page 16)

More traditional media, such as television, has its own shortcomings when it comes to news. Too often television "news" is little more than a video tabloid: lots of hype, lots of sordid detail, and little substance. One need look no further than O.J. Simpson's Bronco escapade several years ago, or Dan Rather's fall from grace to confirm this. One missing girl in Aruba gains national attention, while daily our soldiers are killed and wounded in Iraq. Good news doesn't draw audiences to TV stations; celebrity scandal, falls from grace, and sensationalism do. Who created this environment? Who knows? But it's an awful statement on our society.

As you will soon see, most of the "information" that you have acquired has come from the mass media in one way or another. It has been the "vision" for you, a vision that has come from the outside, not the inside. One of the first steps in creating your own luck is to start drawing the design for your life and to begin to create your *own* visions and your *own* rules. These will be visions and rules that come from *inside* of you, not from the outside. You'll need to think about a few questions for yourself, distinguish your responses from outside influences, and be certain you're answering the questions from the inside:

1. Where did your foundation come from? What does your foundation tell you about your place in the world?

2. What have you learned about relationships? And how has that formed your relationships?

3. How do you get your news and information—and then form your opinions, both as a citizen and a consumer?

The sections that follow will provide some help along the way.

KNOW YOUR FOUNDATION

What are the foundations of your life? They are the ideas of where and how you are to be in the world. They are the things that you know—or at least think you know—about the outside world. They encompass your values, customs, habits, and beliefs.

Where did your foundations come from? The foundations of life are not the things you learned in school. Assuming you were paying attention back then, what you got in school was content—how to add and subtract, the capitals of the states, the basics of research, and all that. Did you get the foundations of your life from your parents? To a certain extent, probably. But given the nature of the dynamics between kids and parents and given the fact that your parents were most likely spending so much time out of the house trying to make a living, it's likely there are gaps. Like your parents, you probably built a portion of your foundations of life from the available media. It's the *percentage* of the foundation that may have come from media that has changed over time. In addition—and unlike your parents—the available media in *your* life has been dramatically different, creating more of a worldview for you. Witness the earlier comparison between my upbringing in the far outskirts of the Poconos, isolated from the rest of the world, and yours, hooked in via the Internet and other media.

When you think about your foundations, have you considered what part advertising has played? Advertising wants to sell you a solution to a problem you didn't think you had. It is not by chance that advertising plays on people's insecurities.

Advertising is also about the intersection of what is being sold with the little voice in your head, the acquisitive, baby voice that says, "I want, I want, I want." This is not your inner voice of wisdom. When the product being advertised (or the way it's advertised) and that voice are in alignment, you're much more apt to buy the product. Consider the tagline in the many advertisements and commercials for prescription drugs: "Ask your doctor about …" More and more patients are showing up in doctors' offices with problems that they may not have known they had. Now, thanks in large measure to advertising, people think they have the advertised ailments and that they can be cured—with the advertised drug. And for the record, all of this cynicism about advertising is coming from someone who made his career out of convincing the public (through advertising) that Men's Wearhouse was the absolute best place to shop for men's clothing. (It is, by the way.)

When you think about your foundations, what parts have television programs, movies, the Internet, and other technologies played? To begin with, television shows, from cartoons to comedy to drama, have taught you that messing up all of the time is okay (think *Friends* and *Seinfeld*). You've learned (if you hadn't already learned this from your parents, or their siblings, or your siblings) that relationships are disposable. Over half of marriages in the real world end in "bail," and any number of TV *comedies* (!) have divorce as their premise, perhaps reflecting just how thoroughly the notion of "work or bail" has been baked into the national psyche. How's that for a not particularly great message for you and the rest of the TV audience?

You've learned that violence is endemic, acceptable, and an answer that many people choose. One need look no further than the entire *CSI* series of shows to see widespread violence and the high-tech ways the "good guys" find the bad guys.

What is the message in *The Simpsons, Family Guy*, or *South Park?* One message is that if you dress the players up as cartoon characters, there is no limit to what they can say, do, or think. There is no limit to tasteless, unsophisticated, ignorant, coarse, unrefined, demeaning, or simply vulgar (take your pick) characterizations of sex, religious beliefs, or ethnic backgrounds. Lest you think that I'm an old curmudgeon, I watch these shows myself; my point here is what the *message* of these shows is. Just because it's accepted on TV doesn't mean that it has to be accepted in your personal life. At some point, you have to take responsibility for your actions. So if you're going to embody the value system of another person, maybe that person ought to be someone other than Homer Simpson.

What have you learned from the "reality" programs? How real are they, *really?* How often are you in contact with the kinds of people you see on *Survivor* or *The Jerry Springer Show?* What is the message and redeeming social value in *American Idol* and similar programs? The real message is how we as a people can fall head over heels dreaming someone else's dream.

Now is a good time to take a step back from the Internet, technology soup, and the television and challenge yourself. Begin to change how you look at your foundation. Ask yourself the following questions:

1. When I think about who I am, is that thought, that vision, something that I have created or is it something that has been created for me? (It doesn't matter who created it; what matters is that *you* know who did.)

2. When I daydream about my life, both now and in the future, what does that look like? And how close is that to my reality?

By asking these questions and developing your answers, you're working on the design of your life and moving yourself steps closer to luck by design. Since chances are good that in your daydreams you are not alone, either in your personal life or your home life, the next questions have to do with relationships.

What about Relationships?

Most human beings need to feel they are part of something. This basic need for love and guidance begins in infancy, through instinct. It soon becomes a genuine want, as we try to create our space in the world and feel like we're part of something bigger than ourselves. At first, we're part of a nuclear family. We all came from some sort of family, and no matter how functional or dysfunctional it was, this family has been a driving force in our lives. It has molded us in many ways, made us who we are, and helped to create our worldview. This foundation is what we bring into every other relationship in our lives, whether the relationship is a friendship, an intimate relationship, or a working relationship.

What Does Advertising Have to Do with Relationships? Like it or not, mass media has played a role and may have helped to distort your vision of relationships. When you think about relationships, what part does advertising play? To begin with, it has influenced how we look at ourselves and others in a purely superficial way. We're constantly bombarded with advertising messages suggesting that we'll look better if we wear this, smell like that, whiten our teeth, color our hair, and lose weight—in short, if we use the advertisers' products. We're being told that—no matter how we look—we either don't measure up, or that we could always look better. When was the last time you saw a clothing model who wasn't svelte and beautiful or handsome and buff? So we find ourselves constantly trying to look like the picture of the stars and the models the advertisers make look most appealing, instead of simply looking like ourselves.

As a result, we walk *into* potential relationships, whether intimate or social, with an unbalanced and unrealistic sense of how we really want and need to look at *ourselves*. A fundamental insecurity is almost inherent. Is it any wonder that relationships fail?

What Role Has Technology Played in Your Vision of Relationships? Stop and think about these two words: *relationship, communication*. Really. **Stop!** Think about the words. What comes to mind? Think of three or four people in your life with whom you would describe yourself as having a relationship. How do you communicate with them? What does that communication look like? If the answer to the latter is all about emails and text messaging, here's a challenge for you: begin to evaluate your current notion of relationships. Relationships and communication are about human interaction—look, feel, and emotion—real senses, in real time. Relationships are also about human beings *relating* to other human beings—looking them in the eye, watching their reaction, and listening to their inflections in sentences. It is through this direct communication that we find the soul qualities in ourselves and in others.

Mankind is pre-wired for relationships, and it's how we have evolved over millions of years. Those who are *not* pre-wired to communicate (people with disorders in the autism spectrum) are the exceptions; their difficulties reading social signals underscore the comparative ease with which most of us navigate social situations. For the most part, nature has seen to it that we learn more about life and more about ourselves when we are *in* relationships, and no amount of technology is ever going to replace that.

How often have you had to backtrack on an email or text message because the recipient totally missed what you were trying to say? Compare that to how often that has happened in face-to-face conversations. There is more to relationships and communication than IMs and text messaging. And, truth be told, there's not a lot of emotion in an emoticon. In fact, it's the contrary: emails and the like cannot take the place of communication, real emotion, real confluence, real contact, and perhaps even real confrontation. Every now and then it's good to get out from behind—from behind the cell phone, the Internet, the video games, and the TV. Get into the street—the living, the feeling, the touching, the smells, and the sounds of the real world. You don't have to abandon technology and virtual reality; just learn to understand and experience the tangible aspects of reality, and know that they count for something.

What Is Your Vision of Relationships? In my research and in my interaction with seventeen- to forty-year-olds, I have sensed a genuine sense of isolation—an isolation that many of them cannot voice. This isolation might have come from the fact that both parents were working and that often they (and any siblings) came home to an empty house. Perhaps the isolation came from the amount of time spent in front of a TV, a video game, or at a computer as a child. This was an amount of time enormously larger than any time their parents might have spent in front of a TV or (less likely) a computer. The sense of isolation tags along every day with the anonymity of Internet sites such as MySpace and Facebook. It has all become part of the current generation.

MySpace, Facebook, and similar sites—what are they about? I've been told that they're about people reaching out for "genuine" interaction. Really? How genuine is it if you're throwing it all out there for everyone, anyone, or no one to see? How genuine is it if instead of creating the persona you are, you can—and might—create an entirely different person? When you meet someone face to face, there is no chance to hide the physical flaws. When you speak to someone face to face, there isn't much of a chance that you're going to hide internal flaws, either. Flaws are more an internal creation, and you're never really going to be able to hide them for long. Flaws are part of the human condition. You've been trained by the media not to accept them, but to cover them up, or disguise them. The media is not helping you. Instead, evaluate for yourself, accept what you want, and choose to change what you want. It's *your* life—take control over it.

If you frequent these sites, take a moment to **stop!** Think about the following: how do you feel when you're "interacting" online versus interacting face-to-face with one of your friends? Is it the same connection? One of the most important lessons to learn is this: you're *not* in this life by yourself—you are alone only if you choose to be. And for the record, you'll be much better off if you choose to be with others, in person, and choose not to be alone and physically isolated. You will learn most things about life and, more importantly, about yourself when you're in relationship. Mankind has evolved and survived for millions of years based on the same premise.

Several years ago, everyone was touting the "new economy" and that in this new economy, there would be little or no paper, everyone would be working from home, and the Internet would make shopping malls obsolete. Look around: I'll bet you have more paper than ever. Certainly no less. Are you working full time from home yet? Unlikely. The malls? Still there. Why? Because no matter what, there is one thing that technology can't overcome: the need for fundamental interconnectedness among people. We want tangible realities, not the ethereal. Whether it's in the form of paper, or a co-worker, or the social experience of shopping together, we want *tangible* experiences.

And whether it's in the workplace or at home, we all need *someone*. We all want to be connected to another person and another thing—

someone and something more and bigger than just ourselves. This is true in our personal lives and in our work lives.

I discovered a chilling exception to this back in 2006, when I attended an event and sat next to the founder and chairman of a very high-profile and successful Internet business. This company has one of the largest and most well-known sites, one that touts "connectivity" and "relationship." I casually mentioned that I was writing a book and said that I thought that it would be helpful for me if I could talk to the employees of the company, figuring that many of them would be in their twenties and thirties. I asked questions to try to find out more about them—where they lived, their age, experience, interests, and more. The CEO then proceeded to inform me (and proudly, I must add) that he had absolutely no idea about any aspect of his employees; he hadn't met 99 percent of them. Further, he told me that he felt no need to or interest in doing so. I was stunned and continue to be. The attitude may work for this particular person— for now—but I wonder how well it works for the employees of the company. What I can tell you is that this is *not* the way to run a business, and it's not a way to run your life.

Do you want to find out who you really are or how you're doing in the world? Look around. See who you're hanging out with. Talk one-on-one, in person, with another human being. There are reasons people—or most people—are hard-wired for personal interaction, and one of them is this: the way we get to know ourselves and draw out soul qualities is through relationships. In short, there are times for the Internet and times to interact directly, in person.

> *The way we get to know ourselves and draw out soul qualities is through relationships.*

The World Out There

While it has yet to reach expectations of many, the Internet has changed the world, in ways large and small. It's part of our world—and I encourage you to reconsider how you use it. Use it as *a* source for your news of the world—just not *the* source. Use it to help you research. With the Internet, you can easily check out the differences between the same news story as reported by several different media sources. That can help you tease out the bias and help you develop a reasoned point of view. And keep doing it. Don't make the mistake some do by reading only the sources that you agree with. Get to know what the "other side" is thinking and saying. Make doing so a practice. The more you know about the "other side," the better. Keep learning so you can see the same issue from your side, the "other side," and even the additional sides you might not have known were out there.

Coming a little closer than your view of the world and international events, consider how you make decisions as a consumer. What is your source of information when it comes to you, as a person making purchases? What does this outside world tell you? Regardless of what medium you access, every day you are subjected to hundreds of advertising messages, many of which are so subtle that they don't register on a conscious level. In fact, even if you don't actively access *any* medium, there are still advertising messages all around you in the form of billboards, bus boards, and advertising that is on all packaging. The messages implore you to buy, buy, and buy. And, in one way or another, the messages all promise the same thing: to make your life better than it currently is.

While it may be obvious on the surface that your life isn't going to change at all by buying *anything*, you'd be surprised at how the subtle messages of advertising can get to you. Consider the following choices that you're likely to have faced in your life: what soft drink you might drink, what beer you might drink, where you get your fast food. Did you make those decisions based upon your own personal taste experiences or by the advertising message that you might have seen? Or even because the products showed up in the background on your favorite show (whether you noticed or not)? Product placement advertising is everywhere. More likely than not, your choice had little to do with the end product and a lot to do with the image of the accumulated advertising on your brain.

The reality is that in today's world, we are all victims of the hype that we see every day through every single means of advertising. And, except for those few who are unplugged and avoid the media, we are bombarded with sounds and images that influence our perspective on the world. How do you build a foundation that will work for you and how do you move forward in the world? What does your source of information need to be?

You need to take in a lot of information—as much available information as you can handle—and then you need to find a way to balance the sources and find what is true—for you. This requires you to trust yourself and to trust your abilities. That might seem challenging at the moment, but stay tuned: there's help in the following chapters. In the end, the true source of your information needs to be yourself. Once you have the tools, you'll discover that the solutions and the "truth" are not outside—they are inside.

Get Out of Your Own Way

You are the architect of your destiny, but in order to craft that plan, you also have to understand that you may also be your own worst enemy, armed with the little stories that you tell yourself. These stories have been ingrained in your psyche, some by the mass media and some by the otherwise well-meaning people around you. These stories get in your way more often than you can notice, and they hinder development, limit personal growth, and keep you from being the person you can truly be. You need to develop the technique to learn how to get out of your own way.

One of the best books that I've ever read on the subject is *A Whack on the Side of the Head,* by Roger von Oech. In this book, von Oech talks about the ways we put limits on ourselves, and therefore limits on our creativity. The essence of the book is the "mental locks" that we have arbitrarily made up. These "locks" are the negative, doubting little voices in our heads that prevent us from not only being more creative, but also from finding our true selves. If you can look beyond these locks, you can refine your personal and professional skills by hearing your true voice, overcoming fear, and discovering your areas of expertise and passion.

The "Mental Locks" are as follows:

1. The Right Answer.
2. That's Not Logical.
3. Follow the Rules.
4. Be Practical.
5. Play Is Frivolous.

6. That's Not My Area.

7. Avoid Ambiguities.

8. Don't Be Foolish.

9. To Err Is Wrong.

10. I'm Not Creative. (page 23)

The "whack on the side of your head" that von Oech suggests is to begin to break away from the locks by little steps, by changing, in ever-so-subtle ways, how you conduct your everyday life. The "Right Answer" lock says a lot about von Oech's wisdom. With numerous examples, he illustrates how people tend to look for one right answer, discarding or ignoring others in their quest for *the* answer. But those who look beyond the obvious find more. He reminds us that Gutenberg used a wine press for an entirely different purpose, and that Picasso turned a bicycle seat into art.

Similarly, many of us go through life thinking that eventually the "right" or "perfect" opportunity will come along to rescue us and miraculously change everything for the better. But what if there are plenty of opportunities and we've just plodded right past them because we weren't paying attention? There are opportunities—every day—and only rarely are they accidental. Instead, it's up to each of us to create and recognize our own opportunities by paying attention to our inner voice and to the outer world. That's what designing your own luck is all about.

The most pervasive dis-ease on the planet is the doubt of who we really are and the doubt of our power and potential. Learn how to trust that your knowledge is a valuable resource, and be comfortable in the reality that your knowledge is often grossly underestimated—mostly by you. No one has lived a life quite like yours. As a result, you have acquired experiences, knowledge, insight, and creativity that can be evolved, developed, and improved. Your unique insights far outweigh the degrees and honors listed on your resume. In every situation, professional and personal, you bring *something* to the scenario that varies from the next person. Stop selling yourself short. Be bold, be confident, even when you're not—for that matter, *especially* when you're not.

I learned this lesson very early, and in a somewhat amusing way, thanks to my Aunt Ethel.

Lesson Learned: Yes, You Can

Aunt Ethel was my father's sister, and an interior decorator who ran a very successful business on the second floor of Boston Hardware. She was tough but kind; worldly, yet a homebody. She approached life with a level of gusto and zeal that was unheard of for a woman in those days. When she wasn't working as a decorator, Ethel was also a painter. Her paintings often were the object of conversation for the rest of the family; I always found them to be colorful, if not interesting. At that point, I had never heard of Monet or Chagall, but the idea of creating something on canvas with paints and brushes intrigued me. Ethel would spend summer weekends camped out in her backyard with paints, brushes, and canvasses—classical music blaring from the record player—loving every minute of it.

One Sunday, when I was about nine years old, I went to spend the day at her house, something I liked to do. There was always an adventure to be had. That day, next to her easel, she had set up another

36

easel with brushes, paint, and a chair—for me.

"Sit down. Paint," she intoned.

"I can't. I don't know how to paint," was my knee-jerk response.

"What do you mean?" she replied. "You have arms, you have hands, and you have eyes. What else do you need?"

So I sat down with Aunt Ethel, and we painted. And while my project looked like a bunch of squiggles and lines, I was just as proud as any "artist" could be. And when Aunt Ethel reminded me to sign my work, I truly felt like I had accomplished something.

Although I couldn't appreciate its importance at the time, Ethel's attitude—her absolute refusal to accept "I can't" as an answer—made its mark. I might have said, "I can't" after that experience, but if so, it wasn't without at least *thinking* about Aunt Ethel and her lesson to me.

It seemed a small moment at the time, but often the biggest impacts come from smallest moments. Then, I had no idea how the simple command to paint could be a first shot in immunizing me against potential mental blocks in my future.

Certainly, overcoming blocks is not a one-shot deal; it takes constant consciousness and work. It's a life-long process—and everything counts.

3

Everything Counts

THIS CHAPTER, PERHAPS MORE THAN any other, is the basis for how you can learn to deal with the experiences and people in your life. It is the basis for how you can identify your authentic self—that person who resides deep down inside of you. That person who, for whatever reason, you may not yet have tapped into. If you get nothing else out of this book, get this chapter.

You weren't born with a personal map of how to traverse through your life; you have to rely on your own resources. You have to rely on your intuition, your trust, your hope, and your ability to deal with the unexpected. There are life lessons in every interaction and in everything you do. And while it's impossible to have your radar turned on and focused at all times, too often, your radar isn't on at all. You must learn to stay awake, to find the meaning, and to learn quickly.

Also—like it or not—you're going to have to create your own solutions. That may sound hard, nearly insurmountable at times, but there are answers. Some, you will learn by paying attention, and by using your radar to learn from each situation and each person. Know that inherent in every problem there resides a ready-made solution. It is your willingness and ability to get quiet and tune into your own self that will help you to find these ready-made solutions. And in the end, because they will be *your own* solutions, they will be worthwhile and enduring life lessons.

How do you tune into your own life and what goes on around you? How do you begin to *wonder* through your life instead of *wandering* through it? How do you begin the path necessary to make your own solutions? How do you establish your own "self"—a self that you can be comfortable with and be proud of? That's the whole point of this chapter, to provide guidance in four main areas, to help you:

1. Be present.
2. Learn to trust yourself and your instincts.
3. Learn how to listen—without your ego.
4. Develop your integrity.

This isn't a shopping list of things "to do"—this is your life list of ways "to be." Work on these areas is continuous. These are not tasks you can complete once and be done with. But by practicing the skills you develop, and using them in your life, you'll be designing your life and creating more positive opportunities; together, these are the foundations to creating your own "luck."

Being Present

The idea of being present exists on a number of levels. The most literal, of course, is to be where you need to be physically at the right time. But being present is far more than this—it's not merely about punching a time clock or raising your hand to let the teacher know you're in attendance. It's truly attending—attending to every moment—at work, in class, with your family, or in your community. Being present is about showing up—with all of your faculties.

Every day, you have a choice—to be actively part of what you're doing or not. You are no longer a child: your mother is not going to push you out the door to go to class. Your own life—every day of it, everything single thing you do—has meaning. Even though up until now you might have approached a new day with the same rote behavior, now would be a good time to stop. Now would be a good time, upon waking up, to really have an awakening—to say to yourself, "*This* is the day."

What is presence? Presence is the ability to sit serenely and in silence and to be aware, alive, and in touch with what is going on *in the moment*, whatever that moment is. It's the ability to quiet the competing voices that are inside your head and outside your body. Presence is learning how to focus on the *one thing* that's in front of you, to get yourself quiet and to quiet the world around you.

Getting quiet with everything that is in you begins by learning how to quiet your own mind—that part of you that is the constant chatter in your life. The chatter is often your personal experience—that endless library of what "was." Instead of opening that library, try to approach every encounter and experience in your life as if it were new. Because guess what? It is. That chatter can also be the source of biases—ones that you are very aware of, and those that you might not even be aware of on a conscious level.

41

What you're faced with in a particular moment might *seem* similar to a previous encounter or experience, but it's not the same. Every day and every situation you encounter is different. You are unique, every person is unique, and every situation is unique. Every situation and every person with whom you interact has to be dealt with *in the moment,* with a sense of attention and detail that is consistent and appropriate *for that moment.* And while it might be nice (not to mention convenient) to deal with every situation and every person the same way, it's just not feasible or wise to do so.

> *You are unique, every person is unique, and every situation is unique.*

The past is clear, but it is nothing more than the journal of where you have been and something that you can't change. The future is some point down a road that you have no way of knowing or controlling. The present is the only thing that you have any control or any power over, and the way to *deal* with the present is by *being* present. By being present, you can learn to quiet the people in your life, many of whom may be trying to help. This doesn't mean to literally shush them, but to recognize their voices and advice when they appear in your head and to balance those voices with your own inner voice. Since no one but you has lived your life, no one but you can be the best judge of what is right for you, what to do, and who to be.

Here's another way to explore the idea of presence. You're no doubt familiar with the kiosks in shopping malls that show the layout of the stores. In order to help you determine where you are relative to the stores, the signs typically have a brightly colored X, labeled, "You are here." And yes, you are. Think of your life as a series of Xs—and all you ever are is just "here." As you're reading this, you are "here" too. And you'll still be "here" for the next thing that you do. And if you keep repeating to yourself, "I am here," you'll be that much closer to practicing presence.

Take a moment to try a little experiment. ***Stop!*** Do you remember what you read three pages ago? Think about it for a moment and then go back and check it out. If you couldn't remember, then you weren't practicing presence; instead, you were reading words while your mind was engaged in something else. Make it a habit to stop periodically and ask yourself if you've just paid attention to the last thirty minutes of your life. If you had to, could you relate to someone else what you had done for those last thirty minutes? If it all just "slipped by," then you're not practicing presence.

Can you be "present" all of the time? Of course not—that's why it's called "practicing" presence. To help you practice, try every now and then to look inside yourself in a physical, not mental, way. Stop and notice how you are breathing: are you taking short, quick breaths, or is your breathing long and deliberate? What is your posture like? Do you have to do something different in order to be present? Are you doing more than one thing at a time?

When you notice that you're *not* present, here's a quick way to bring yourself back to the now:

Open your hands and spread your fingers, palms facing each other. Touch opposite fingertips together, all at the same time. Repeat a few times. Sometimes the simple act of feeling your own skin can reconnect you to yourself and to the present moment.

If all of this seems like I'm trying to sneak in a little meditation and yoga, you're absolutely right. Both are excellent practices to help mind and body—and will be covered in more detail later in the book. For now, I'll rely on a little teaser from *Yoga Mind, Body & Spirit* by Donna Farhi: "Yoga is a technology for arriving in this present moment. It is a means of waking up from our spiritual amnesia, so that we can remember all that we already know" (page 5).

I can't overstate the importance of being present. Once you are able to be fully present and to access your inner wisdom, your life will change and take on new depth. Being present enables you to see and to really understand that for every action there is a reaction. You see that when you treat someone with respect, that person—whether it's someone you know or someone you encounter on the street—reciprocates with respect. It becomes clear that in order to get respect, you have to give respect. Plus, it's the right thing to do. And you just never know: the people you pass on the way up might be the same ones you see on the way down. What goes around comes around. Sounds like a cliché, you might be thinking. Well, it might be, and it's the truth. Treat everyone with respect; you'll not regret it. In a similar fashion, you see that in order to be trusted, you have trust yourself and be trustworthy.

Trusting Yourself and Your Intuition

Before you can *trust* your intuition, you have to *discover* your intuition. How do you go about it? Step one is to recognize that intuition isn't a thing. It's something that is in your heart and your soul, not in your head. *It's a voice. Things* are easy to find—car keys, the laundry, or a golf ball. *Voices* are much more difficult to isolate. But when you're paying attention—when you are present—the voices are more obvious than any golf ball. The voices can range from the ones that are encouraging you to the ones that are second-guessing you. Sometimes the voices are those of chaos, crisis, and confusion. Sometimes they can be the voices of truth and trust.

The voices of chaos, crisis, and confusion are generally a lot louder. They come from your mind as it is constantly reviewing information and passing judgment based on "experience." This feedback from your brain is part of human nature, but these voices are rarely helpful. *Now* is the time to learn how to change that part of your humanness. The voices of truth and trust are much softer because they are much closer to your heart and have nothing to do with your mind. Learning how to tune out the multitude of voices and finding and listening to the *one* that's worthwhile can be a daunting task, but by getting quiet and being present, it becomes a lot easier.

Unlike instincts, which are innate, intuition can be thought of as both innate and learned. The innate portion of your intuition is an internal gift from a much more evolved part of you that's plugged into your own "grand design." You might not be always aware of it on a completely conscious level, but on some level, you do know it is there. Tuning in to your intuition involves tuning out the unhelpful voices and practicing presence.

Step two of discovering and trusting your intuition is to learn about trust. And what about trust? Trust is the number one ingredient in every single relationship in your life—especially your relationship with yourself. Before you can even begin to *think* about trusting others, you're going to have to trust yourself. Learning to have trust in yourself is a matter of trial and error and discovering how to learn from past mistakes. The key is to *remember* the past mistakes and the lessons they taught you. Here's an example that you might have experienced as a child, or if not, you can certainly imagine it. Pointing your finger or wielding a stick or pencil, you were drawn toward an electrical socket, as if you were on a mission. Observant child that you were, you'd seen other people put things into similar sockets with seemingly positive results. Your curiosity said, "Me too!" Well, unless someone older and wiser swooped in to intercede, sparks flew—and you probably weren't going to try *that* again.

Now think of the last time you made a mistake—choose a really big one. What do you remember about it? Was there a chance that before you made the mistake, there was a little voice that was telling you to do something other than what you ended up doing? Did you ignore that voice? No problem; it happens. However, in thinking about that mistake, what did you learn from it? Did you take the time then to stop and ask yourself what you had learned? The most important thing you can do after making a mistake is to stop, look, and learn. What went wrong? How did it go wrong? And what can you do to prevent that from happening again? These are good questions and questions for which only *you* have the answer.

So, put it together—intuition and trust—how do you develop the wherewithal to trust your intuition? There is only one way: through trial and error, experimentation and learning by making mistakes, and by reflecting upon the successes and knowing *why* you succeeded.

Yes, the younger we are, the more we rely without reservation on our instincts and trust. However, innocence does not equal ignorance. Quite the contrary—our youthful innocence allows us to be much more free in our experimentation. In retrospect, I see that I had a very powerful lesson about intuition and trust when I was just barely a teenager.

BE QUIET, DON'T WORRY

I was a very quiet child. *Very* quiet. It wasn't because I didn't have anything to say. I just couldn't really find my platform, and the constant comparisons to my siblings further complicated my search to find my place. It wasn't until the night of my bar mitzvah—December 6, 1963—that I had an opportunity to find that platform. For nearly a year, I'd prepared for the event with diligence, yet with a certain rote sameness that neither intrigued nor intimidated me. I was thirteen years old. At that age, everyone I knew had a bar mitzvah. It was the standard coming of age celebration within the Jewish community. In my world, it was no big deal.

Two weeks prior to my big event, President John F. Kennedy had been assassinated in Dallas. Everyone I knew and everyone I looked at was in a state of complete shock: this was a surreal experience in universal grief that I had never before witnessed. The heartbeat of the world had stopped, and the shine of America seemed to dull. It was also the first time in history that a national tragedy was played out on the new medium of television. Kennedy's assassination—its very occurrence, its visibility, and the fact that anyone within range of a television knew of the events practically as they played out—changed the sense of isolation. And of innocence. As best as a thirteen-year-old could, I tried to separate this universal grief from my own sense of joy and excitement. I knew that the crowd at temple two weeks later would be gathered there because it was *my* bar mitzvah. I hoped they would focus on my every word in rapt attention. On this one night, *my night*, there would be no comparison with my sister or brother. I was sure of that.

As my parents, rabbi, and I sat behind the pulpit waiting for services to begin, there was an air of tension that was clear, but not spoken. A few minutes before we were to sit in front of the congregation, my mother turned to me and asked where my notes were. I had kept a package of papers that included the translations, the Hebrew, and my speech. It had been part of my daily routine for several months; however, bringing all of that with me on that night had not even occurred to me. "What for?" I thought. "I know all of this stuff." I turned to my mother and told her that the notes were at home. The fright visible in her face was perfectly counterbalanced by the calmness in mine. "I don't need them," I replied. "I know what I'm doing." Moments later, as I stood in front of the congregation—noteless and calm—I experienced an unfamiliar surge of adrenaline pulsing through me. At the time, I couldn't label the feeling. I didn't understand it, but I knew that it was *something*. It was confidence—*inner confidence*.

Somewhere deep inside, in a place I could barely fathom, let alone trust, I had great instincts and an inner confidence. Of course, as a child, I had no concept of this. And if I'd had a clue, I doubt that I would have understood, appreciated, or trusted any of it. Generally, I was unable to balance the sibling comparisons with my sense of self, and I believed what I had been told up until then: *I just didn't match up.*

But when push came to shove, and all was calm, I was able to employ what would later become an important business and life practice—I got quiet, trusted myself, and allowed my inner confidence to speak. My intuition, which I was beginning to sense, told me where to join and where to flee. My quiet confidence made me the attractive leader of most organizations I joined, yet I rarely knew why at the time. Often, others could see this clearly, while I wondered why. I constantly struggled with leadership qualities that I barely understood and my own inner confidence, which I understood even less. Yet somehow I knew that "quiet" was a good thing for me.

As we get older, we don't necessarily lose our intuition; we lose our *ability* and *willingness* to trust it. Of course, not all experiences are as eye opening as the shocking socket or the affirming bar mitzvah. But every decision you make, every opportunity you have to rely on your instincts and your intuition, is based on your own experience. While experience is an important factor in approaching something new, intuition is the more important factor.

How do you know you're on the right track to something? How do you know when your intuition is serving you well? Watch the flow of your thoughts, feelings, and senses. When they feel like they are all flowing smoothly, you're on track. If you're pushing yourself to get through it, then you're on the wrong track. Your gut tells the truth; your mind, which is not particularly helpful, rationalizes and justifies. Stay close to your gut.

Fortunately, I did so naturally when I went away to college. Unlike many of my friends, I had no earthly idea what I was going to major in or what I was going to *be* when I graduated. At Rutgers, I decided to study what interested me—books. So my answer was to become an English major. While my friends were killing themselves studying organic chemistry, biology, accounting, and American history, I was reading. Reading Hemingway, Fitzgerald, and Faulkner. Mailer, Bellow, and Vonnegut. The reading lists, all of them, were an absolute treat for my brain. As my fraternity brothers were cramming for finals, I was writing papers and expanding my creativity. While I still had no vocational "goal," I just wasn't worried, and I didn't let the concerns of those around me affect me. Somehow, some way, I knew that I'd be fine. Once again, quiet confidence let me be in a comfortable place, despite being surrounded by peers who knew what they were going to be (and were, perhaps, a bit frantic about it).

I recognized college as more than a means to the end of getting a degree: I recognized it as a time to experiment, to explore, and to have an all-around good time. When academic life became less than a challenge, I found a way to earn money in my spare time—and without a boss. Who would have known that selling sweaters out of my fraternity room was a beginning step to my career?

Sweater City: An Adventure in Trust

In my sophomore year of college, I spent my bar mitzvah money to buy a '69 Volvo. Between the car upkeep, occasional trips to New York, and my phone bills, I soon needed to make some extra cash.

The father of a friend of mine from high school owned a men's shirt and sweater factory back in Hazleton. The factory had an outlet store as well, selling overruns and irregulars. When I was at home for spring break, I went to the outlet store to buy a few shirts for myself. While shopping, it dawned on me that if I could get a slight price break on the shirts and sweaters in the outlet store, I might be able to resell them at school. On the spot, I negotiated a price for the purchase of as many shirts and sweaters as could fit in my Volvo, and I was in business. With more confidence than money, I wrote a check, knowing full well that it wouldn't clear. But I also knew that as soon as I got back to New Brunswick, I'd be able to sell enough shirts to at least cover it. This marked the beginning of my first solo retail venture, and my first venture in the clothing business.

The message? Blind faith trumps that doubting voice that says, "No way." I didn't think twice about writing that check. I never worried about the consequences of what might happen if it bounced. My motivation was partly experimentation and partly fear—fear of not having enough money for all that I wanted to do. I trusted my instincts over the reality of my meager checking account balance. I realized who I was and what I could do. And I was right. There were lessons for me here that I carried with me long past my college days.

Learning to Listen—Without Your Ego

A terrific quality to develop and a most underused skill in everyday life or at work is a fundamental understanding of human nature. That understanding begins by listening. From a place of listening, you can build rapport and be able to respond to the people around you in a meaningful way—with integrity and with a sense of trustworthiness. You can't account for the place that someone else is coming from; you can only account for your own place. When you listen with your heart and acknowledge your intuitive power, you gain confidence, direction, and courage. And by listening with your heart, you do a tremendous service to the person who is talking to you.

Perhaps you're murmuring to yourself, "I hear what other people have to say all of the time." But think about that for a second. There's a *big* difference between hearing and listening. Hearing is a sense that most of us are born with. The frequency, intensity, and duration of a sound travel through auditory nerve fibers to the brain, allowing our body to process and interpret these signals. That's all very nice but very mechanical. Listening, on the other hand, is not a sense, and it's not mechanical; it is a trait that you have to develop. Here's a practical approach to listening. You know that you want to be heard. If you want to be heard, learn how to listen. Although this sounds simple, it's far from it. Listening requires practice, and it requires presence. Learning how to listen is an art, not a science—you aren't going to learn how to do it unless you *practice* listening.

That said, I'll offer some information and practical reminders that should help. No doubt you're well aware that we all spend a great deal of the day communicating in one form or another. But how much of that communicating involves listening? Unfortunately, not nearly enough. To help yourself get quiet and learn how to listen, make it a practice to assume that there is more information in front of you than inside you. You already know what you already know. What you *don't know* is what the other person knows. If you can learn to control your mouth and keep your mind from wandering, you'll be able to learn much more by *just listening*.

ALL KNOWLEDGE IS NEW

You're not born with knowledge; it's something you attain throughout life. And we all attain different facts at different times in our lives. Be patient with others in their goals to attain new knowledge. That's a lesson I learned by example—a very unpleasant one.

Many years ago, I was thrust into a situation in which I instantly became the dress shirt buyer for Men's Wearhouse. I was young and unprepared, and my first buying trip to New York was the day after I became the shirt buyer. I knew absolutely nothing about dress shirts other than the fact that I wore one every now and then. I met with a vendor who had been selling shirts to Men's Wearhouse for a few years, but of course he hadn't been selling shirts to *me*. He was showing me patterned dress shirts and said something about "woven" and "print" shirts. I had no idea what the difference was, and in the moment, without regard to the consequence of my question, I asked what the difference was. In *his* moment, he was stunned at my ignorance and gave me a several-minute lecture about how stupid I was that I didn't know the difference. (And yes, he did use the word "stupid.") As I sat there being berated by this person, it dawned on me that at some point in *his* life, *he* hadn't known the difference between a print and a woven shirt, either. I knew for sure that neither one of us had been born with this information, and the only difference between us was when we acquired it. I refused to let him make me feel "less than," thanked him for the clarity and the lesson, and moved on.

To listen effectively, you must be *actively* involved in the communication process. It's so simple, yet for so many, so elusive. If you take the lessons you've already learned about practicing presence and apply them to the tips below, you'll become an able listener, a better friend and colleague to those who are talking to you, and best of all, you'll open your mind to those things you might not have thought about or even truly heard before.

TIPS FOR BETTER LISTENING

As Samuel Clemens (that's Mark Twain, again) said: "If we were supposed to talk more than we listen, we would have two mouths and one ear." Unfortunately, most of us conduct our lives as if we *do* have two mouths and one ear. The most natural thing for most of us is to *not* listen. Our world is filled with information, and we move very quickly—most of the time too quickly to stop and just listen. But it doesn't make it right. As you read the tips that follow, spend time thinking about each one. They may well be new ideas to you and might force you to rethink what you've thought until now. They'll also make you a better listener and better friend to those to whom you're listening.

Use the Five-Minute Rule. Whether it's in business or in your personal life, how many times has someone come to you with an idea that, at first blush, you rejected? How many times, during that mental rejection and while the other person was still talking, did you begin to formulate your reasons for thinking that the idea wasn't a good one and completely ignored what the other person was saying?

The next time, try this: for at least five minutes, approach every outside idea as a good one—as a great one—and think of ways that you can build on, rather than destroy, that idea. There's always a time and a place for rejection. The seeds of a good idea are best cultivated when the idea is still new and fresh, when there is still excitement in the heart and voice of the creator. Albert Einstein, certainly an advocate of new ideas, said, "For an idea that does not first seem insane, there is no hope." So, no matter how wild the idea, don't bash it; embrace it. You'd want the same thing if it were *your* idea.

Be Calm and Receptive. Always assume that you're getting information that is new to you. Don't let your mind start rummaging through the old files in your memory bank to find what may be familiar about the information that you're hearing. It may be *familiar*, but it's not the *same*. Your mind and your ego might also be telling you that what you are hearing is "incorrect" in an effort to protect any hidden prejudices and closed-minded opinions. But it's only your mind playing the "same old, same old" game with you, a game that prevents you from hearing what is said. So be present and let everything you hear be new. Use that five-minute rule and let it seem correct for at least those few minutes.

Be Quiet and Don't Interrupt. From a place of quietness, you can tap into your soul and expand your mind. In order to be quiet, you have to be calm. (In order to be calm, see above.) Your desire to put your own information out there should be tempered by your desire to listen and wait your turn. Let the other person have his say. Hopefully, he'll be able to watch you and your listening style, appreciate it, and do so the same when it's his turn to listen. Pay special attention if something pops up to you as the "dumbest" or the "most outrageous" thing—the thing that you *least* agree with. Guess what? There is someone on the other side with as much positive passion about their belief and point of view as you.

Pay Attention. It's natural to be working on your response at the same time as you are listening. Stop doing this! If you're "listening" and simultaneously formulating your response, you're violating all of the above rules. How? Listening to someone else and talking to yourself at the same time is chaotic, which is the opposite of calm. And if you're talking to yourself while listening to someone else, you're interrupting, in a way. Granted, you're not making audible sounds, but there is plenty of noise—in your head. You're talking, just not out loud. Clearly, you're a far more effective listener when you're not talking. It's not the worst thing to first listen and then have an actual pause in the conversation before you respond.

Leash Your Ego. Here's what is, for many, the most difficult tip. Put your ego away. Think of it as the accumulation of all of the mental garbage that you have collected over the course of your lifetime. Lock it in a drawer. At least keep it leashed. Why? We can only *really* hear others to the degree we can hold, contain, acknowledge, and validate ourselves. Personal validation begins with winning the battle with the ego and becoming comfortable in your own skin.

Imagine if I had taken seriously what that dress shirt vendor said to me about my brainpower. Instead of listening to what he told me about shirts (after having berated me), I'd have been defensive and tending to my battered ego. Chances are I couldn't have absorbed all the information and would have had a hard time continuing the task at hand, which was buying shirts. The lesson? If you are unsure about yourself, or unsure about a specific belief that you might have, it's going to be very hard for you to hear that belief challenged, to ask questions, or to gain new information. If you are unsure, *ask questions.*

Need a little more reason to leash your ego? Think about ego and realize that it has more than one gear. It can be in neutral, moving forward, or going in reverse. When you remove your ego from a situation, you are admitting that someone else has something to say and has a point of view. (That's your ego in neutral.) Sometimes that new point of view doesn't agree with yours. (Reverse.) But what someone else has to say *counts!* It's a point of view, albeit sometimes not *your* point of view. If you are truly in a relationship, there's plenty of time to promote your own point of view. (Forward.) As you probably were told in kindergarten, *wait your turn.* Keep your ego in neutral (leashed). When you have your ego in neutral, treating others with respect comes more naturally.

Life Is Often Like a Poker Game

Life is not like one of those poker games on the Internet, but the kind where real human beings sit down at a real table and play with real money. True, there are gambles involved in both, and human interaction, but why talk about poker when the topic is learning how to listen? Poker is not entirely about gambling on the cards—it's about observing physical actions and listening to what's going on at the table with the other players. If you try to watch it all, you will almost certainly become frustrated, fail, and observe nothing, not to mention not winning anything. The trick is to balance a variety of information, and to focus on *one thing* at a time. It is not enough to just "see" the betting patterns. You have to constantly recognize the behavior of your opponents, know intuitively when they are bluffing or have a good hand, and truly capitalize on that information. Of course, watching your own hand and having a basic understanding of your own odds in a given situation is important, but what distinguishes the great poker players from the not-so-great and the difference between poker on the Internet and "live" poker is the human connection.

My poker-playing days at Rutgers taught me that you could learn just as much from watching the players as you can from the cards. And those lessons were very worthwhile: my frequent winnings helped pay my way through college. I was able to become keenly aware of the motivation and body language of the people I played with, and was thereby able to move the odds slightly in my favor. Paying attention also enabled me to not make the same mistakes twice—something I noticed the others at the table doing constantly. It's not that I got better cards or started out with better skills. But I stayed with the game and focused primarily on playing poker. And when their attention drifted to drinking and joking around, my fellow card players made enough mistakes that my odds increased still more. We all had a good time, but by focusing on the one thing that counted, I controlled my game and increased my chances.

Essentially, good poker playing is more about discovering how to learn by observing habits. Poker is not just a skill. It's an art in learning how to turn up your listening and intuitive skills, and reading between the lines. If you can quiet your ego, pre-conceived judgments, and feelings of self-doubt, you'll be surprised by what you see and hear in poker and—more importantly—in life.

Establishing Integrity in Your Life

Integrity is the powerful force behind what you say and what you do. It's the most vital piece of who you are and who you will ever become. Integrity is the intersection of your systems of beliefs and your value systems. Having integrity means living your life with honesty, honoring your word and beliefs, and taking responsibility for your actions. It is the result of thinking, making decisions, and opting for the right motives. It's about vision and judgment of the person who practices it. It's about doing good for the sake of doing good—when no one is watching—and without expecting recognition. You do it because the behavior outwardly reflects your beliefs and is woven into the fabric of your being, beliefs, and values and frames the way you consciously want to lead your life. It's the person who distributes two hundred homemade lunches every month to the homeless at the train station on his lunch hour. It's the person who pays a debt that may have been long forgotten by someone else. Or the person who shovels her elderly neighbors' walkways so they can get out and about safely. It's conducting yourself a certain way, not because your mother told you so, or to earn a pat on the back.

Like learning to listen or trusting your instincts, establishing your integrity requires risks, uncertainty, practice, and continual mental effort. The risk and uncertainty come from the fact that establishing and sustaining your integrity might mean that you're going to be at odds with someone else. You might have to call people on their behavior or ethics; you might have to go as far as to sever a friendship or a business relationship because you're at a fundamental crossroads. The practice and mental effort might be a chore at first, but with time, they'll come naturally. It's an effort that's worthwhile and essential, no matter what the cost.

Any time you compromise your integrity, you've essentially lost the most important character trait you have. Any time you fail to do what you *know* in your heart or in your soul is right, deep down inside you lessen your self-worth, impede your outlook on the world, and damage your ability to live a happy life. Your goals can become harder to reach, you attract people who make you feel bad, and you lose your trust in yourself.

Instead, be honest. Know that everything you do and everything you say sculpts your character. There is no such thing as a "little" lie—any non-truth gets embedded in your psyche.

Lie detectors are great at monitoring what happens to your inner body when you tell a lie. Absent the lie detector, try an experiment of your own. Watch what happens to your outer body the next time you try one of those "little lies." Your breathing might change and become more shallow. Or if you're talking to another person, you might stop making eye contact. You might even have trouble just sitting or standing without being fidgety. The honest soul in each of us refuses to allow a lie to go unnoticed. But over time, that soul does have the flexibility to allow us to learn to lie. If you get comfortable with the "little" lie, you'll be that much less uncomfortable with the slightly larger lie. The more lies, the easier the next one becomes; and then the next may be slightly larger, larger, and larger still. This is clearly not the kind of flexibility that one can be proud of.

Studies have shown that our brains register and remember everything we do. Our ability to *recall* any one thing in the moment is the difference between good and poor memory. It's not too much of a leap, therefore, to assume that the same holds true for little lies versus any other kind of lie. Little untruths leave an imprint on the soul, just as the larger ones do. The bottom line? Learn to tell the truth: be honest. It's the right thing to do—for your soul and for your physical well being.

There is no denying it: your life is the sum and substance of what you put into it. No one deserves the credit for the things you've done well other than you. By the same token, no one else deserves the blame. While it is often convenient and ego soothing to assign blame when something goes wrong, often there is no blame, and there are no victims.

Similarly, there are no shortcuts or easy ways, and you rarely "get away" with anything. You are going to have to work to get the things you want. That work might be long and laborious, but when you do the work, you'll feel much better at the end of the process, knowing that you didn't take the easy way out. If you take what appears to be a shortcut, you might *think* you've gotten away with something, but you haven't. Sooner or later, everything catches up with you. Whether it's something as simple as wasting your time on the supposed shortcut or as complicated as making a large mistake that you're going to have to unravel at a later date, what you do will reflect on you. Thanks to the Internet, even your online posts and YouTube videos can follow you into the future. Be aware of what you're projecting into the world, both in what you do and don't do. Shun the shortcut. Behave as you wish to be known, and not just for today.

Work, don't bail. When a problem arises, your initial instinct might be to bail—to abandon—whether it's in a relationship or some other issue that needs to be solved. Decide now to *work*. Bailing without working is the easy way out, and like lying, it can become habitual if you don't watch it. There is nothing to be gained from walking away from a problem. If the problem becomes a failure, *that's* where the gain comes—in learning from the failure. (For more on that subject, see chapter 5.)

At a dinner that I hosted with about twenty members of my advisory board, we discussed the notion of bailing. About half of those present felt they had been well trained on the notion of bailing, by parents whose relationship didn't work out and ended in divorce. It was hard for me to argue that specific case of bailing, having been guilty myself, but I tried.

I certainly know that there were times that I could have walked away from Men's Wearhouse. We went through some very trying years when all of our hard work amounted to little more than financial loss, and the easy way out might have been to sell off the company to another one in better financial shape. But rather than bail, George and I and the rest of the management team decided to redouble our efforts. Why? We had two big reasons. One, we believed in ourselves and in what we were doing and knew that with time, we'd be able to improve the company. Two, we realized that we had our hopes and dreams and those of hundreds of employees at stake as well. There were a lot of people counting on us. Bailing (as in selling the company) might have been easier, but it wasn't the right thing to do. For us, the decision became more like the notion of bailing a cherished boat that had taken on water. We knew that the store and the employees were worth the effort, and we weren't about to let them sink or drift away.

It was the Buddha who once said, "How you do anything is how you do everything." And indeed, that's the consistent thread that runs through these recommendations to be honest, be accountable, shun the shortcut, and work rather than bail. It comes down to this: Be aware of your actions. Be aware that how you do anything *is* how you do everything. Think about it also as you watch others. If you can lie about a small thing, you can lie about a bigger thing. Similarly, if you know a friend or associate has issues with the truth, know that you need to be cautious extending your trust. You are accountable, so *be* accountable. Skip the shortcut; don't bail. Value your integrity.

STINKY SUITS: IN SEARCH OF INTEGRITY

In my entire career at Men's Wearhouse, the single most egregious act committed against the company took on its own aroma and became a lesson for many. Beyond this, it bears mentioning as a failure of accountability and integrity that forever changed my view of a particular vendor. It had to do with what came to be known as "stinky suits."

By way of background, you'll need a crash course in the manufacturing of men's suits, so here goes. Before a suit is actually sewn together, the fabric has to be woven, generally at another factory, also known as a piece-goods mill. After the fabric is woven, it is then "sponged." Sponging does what the name implies—a light coat of water mixed with chemicals is applied to the fabric, allowing it to shrink so that shrinkage doesn't occur later on. Enough with the lesson.

One day, I went into our warehouse to look at a delivery of suits from a certain supplier. As I walked around, I noticed an awful smell, like a skunk. Assuming it *was* a skunk, I spoke to the warehouse manager, who mentioned that he also had smelled something, but he couldn't pinpoint the location. We hunted around for a skunk, didn't find one, and we both let it go.

Several weeks later, at a meeting, a few managers commented that they had smelled something odd in their stores. When I asked them what it smelled like, they unanimously responded, "A skunk." So the original "skunk in the warehouse" theory was gone. The question now became this: where was the smell coming from? Again, for lack of any definitive cause, we all had to let it go. A few days later, I received a letter from an irate customer, who explained that he had bought a suit at Men's Wearhouse for a job interview and that en route to the interview, he got caught in a light drizzle. Of course, his suit got wet, but that wasn't his issue. His issue was that by the time the suit dried, it smelled terrible—like a skunk. But he had to go to the interview. And, of course, he didn't get the job.

I quickly found out exactly what suit the man had bought and started to put the pieces together. Not only had he bought a suit from that certain unnamed manufacturer, but he had also bought one of the suits that was in the warehouse on the day that I initially smelled the skunk-like odor. I immediately called the manufacturer, who let me know that I was the first to call with such a problem. Unsure whether to ask for a reward or something, I asked if this crazy notion seemed even plausible. "Of course not," I was told. Two days later, a call came in from another customer with a similar story. Two days after that, three calls came in from three different Men's Wearhouse stores complaining about a foul, overwhelming smell. I made another call to the manufacturer. Once again, the answer was basically, "Not my problem." Except it now *was* a problem, and I was getting very nervous. I immediately called all of the stores and told them to return the suspect suits to our warehouse ASAP. I told the vendor that I was doing so as well. More stonewalling ensued, and I was accused of overreacting.

Fortunately, the manufacturer's sales rep was more cooperative. He flew to our Fremont, California, warehouse, and he and I walked through it, examining and smelling the suits. We pulled a few out, sprayed them lightly with water, and the smell got worse. He then called the manufacturer, and *he* got the run around.

That was the last straw for me. There was no question that the suits were going to be returned. What I wanted to know was is why I got stonewalled, and what exactly had happened. The sales rep agreed and obliged, and through his contacts in the factory, he discovered something astounding. When the piece goods had originally been delivered to the factory, the smell was so overpowering that they had to close down the facility for part of the day. Whether the cause had been the chemical mix or how it had been applied didn't matter; what mattered was that rather than resolve the problem, the manufacturer had ignored it and proceeded to make the suits.

In a roundabout way, and after weeks of no cooperation, the manufacturer recognized that there had been *some* sort of problem. Their quick solution? They wanted to lower the price of the suits to us, so we could lower the price to our customers. Of course, this was no solution. Instead, it just underscored the manufacturer's lack of integrity and accountability.

Bottom line? We didn't pass the suits onto customers— they went right back to the manufacturer. And we learned some valuable lessons:

- How a person or a company responds to adversity is a window on their character and soul. The decision to go ahead and make the suits was made by a middle-level manager. But the ethos of looking the other way was not his—he was no doubt repeating something he had seen at another time, further up the corporate ladder.

- There are people in the world who put their integrity before everything else. The manufacturer's sales rep who worked to get to the cause of the problem did what he believed was right. By choosing not to stonewall or deny, he didn't do the "corporate" thing but went up against his company. And, as a postscript, he didn't last much longer in that company. He did, however, maintain his integrity.

We're all tested at many points in our work and personal lives. Sometimes exercising your integrity can make you unpopular or even cause tangible damage, such as losing your job or losing a friendship. Know that you *can* do good and do business. Integrity in relationships involves responding to and communicating with others—whether it's a co-worker or a close friend—with complete openness and honesty. When truthfulness is paired with integrity, you can make promises that will be respected and have meaning. Personal integrity counts. Similarly, despite corporate scandals that have undermined the public's faith in business, most companies *are* honest, and many do lots of great things.

TIME EXAMINING YOUR MOTIVES IS TIME WELL SPENT

Any time you interact with another person, examine your heart and examine your motives. When you treat people with respect and compassion, you're on stable ground. Remember the Golden Rule: Do unto others as you would have them do unto you. Are you not listening to someone who is talking with you? Have you treated them with contempt? Indifference? Dispassion? It's not only *that* you might be treating them this way; the question is *why*.

You want to really start to change your life? Sit down quietly for a bit and examine your motives. Start with honest self-observation. To transform yourself, start from the inside—the same inside where (once again) all of the answers reside. If you don't, you'll make things more difficult for yourself than they need to be. After trial and error, you'll find that the really hard things in life are resistance and lack of forgiveness and that the really easy things are acceptance, compassion, and kindness. The idea might seem backwards. After all, sticking to your guns no matter what the cost or holding a grudge appears to be easy and require little self-awareness and contemplation. But when you start down the path of practicing acceptance, compassion, and kindness, through self-awareness and contemplation, you'll find yourself moving through life with a little less resistance—from the inside and from the outside.

Here's another way to think about it, and a great piece of advice (even if I do say so). If you're one who highlights and dog ears book pages, do so to this page. The advice is: *Pick up after yourself.* Yep, just like your mother used to say. Except that what I'm really referring to is to pick up the pieces of your life. Remember: you need to be accountable. Accountability is a component of integrity, and it's part of the package of living an authentic existence.

You want to really start to change your life? … Pick up after yourself.

An awful lot has been covered in this chapter, and if you've gotten this far and are a bit dizzy, be patient. The material you've just read is really the foundation for the rest of the book. But at a very basic level, what it all comes down to is two words: "Trust yourself." When you learn to trust yourself, the rest of the pieces of your life begin to fall into place more easily.

Lesson Learned: Trust Yourself

It doesn't matter how or why or when you begin to trust yourself. What's important is that you learn to do so at some point. I'm fortunate to be one of those people who did so at a very young age. Why? I suspect that having had exposure to personal failure at an early age, I was forced to turn inside to the one person I could trust—myself.

As it happened, my early years in Houston were rife with smart decisions based on little more than self-trust. When I returned to Men's Wearhouse from Marcom-Day, George wanted me to stay for good, so he offered to sell me stock in the company. His proposal was to sell me one third of the company for $3,000. While today that amount of money might seem trivial, at the time, and to me, it was not at all trivial. I simply didn't *have* $3,000 to invest, and had few personal assets to use as collateral. I sought the advice of my father, who, working from his own paradigms, tried to talk me out of investing. First, he pointed out that Men's Wearhouse had a negative net worth. I would therefore be investing in a company that was worthless, which it was at the time. So he warned that my investment looked shaky, at best. Second, he believed that not owning 51 percent of something was the same as owning none of it. No more, no less.

Fortunately, I wasn't asking for the favor of borrowing money. I was seeking advice, which I listened to, and then decided to ignore. I knew it was wise to ask for advice—and to make an independent decision. I knew that, in this instance, I had to effectively say, "That's nice, thanks. Now get out of my way." I relied on my instincts and intuition and made a decision contrary to the opinion of a man—

my father—whom I trusted and respected. I had a good feeling in general about the future of Men's Wearhouse, and George Zimmer in particular; that feeling was strong enough to override the advice. In retrospect, this decision, based on strong self-trust, was my smartest business decision—ever.

> *Ask for advice—and make an independent decision ... Know when to say, "That's nice, thanks. Now get out of my way."*

I went to a Houston bank and using my car as collateral, secured a one-year $3,000 loan to become a Men's Wearhouse stockholder. It all felt right. And I certainly had done my homework; I knew the business, having been associated with it in one way or another practically since its inception. Beyond that, what I trusted then was my intuition—not my intellect, my heart, my head, or any outside advisor. I also trusted my own abilities to work hard and make things happen for myself and for what now represented my single largest asset.

For the record, my dad has a great sense of humor in remembering this story and often retells it to friends as well as to me with a big smile on his face. One of the wonders of time is that it changes everything. At the time, my decision to buy Men's Wearhouse stock seemed like a risky one. Over time, the decision was obviously less and less risky.

Time is an important element in our lives, and it's a commodity that has an unknown duration. An integral part to creating your own luck has to do with the way in which you use time, a topic examined in detail in the next chapter.

4

We're All Playing for the Same Thing: Time

TIME AND OUR PHYSICAL HEALTH are the most precious and the most personal assets we have in our lives. While we may have some control over our health, we have no control over our time. We each have a finite amount of it: twenty-four hours each day, 365 days each year. Our total allotment of years might be known—but not to us. It's one of the great mysteries of life. So really, we're all playing for the same thing: time. As it turns out, the bumper stickers are correct: Life is not a dress rehearsal.

Because we're all playing for the same thing, it creates an even playing field. There are no advantages to any one person. And although you have no control over the total amount of time you have in your life, you can exert control over the time that you *do* have control over—the present time. In this chapter, I set forth a number of strategies to help you learn how to make time work for you, instead of the other way around. But first, take a few moments to think about the relativity of time.

71

Time Is Relative

Do you remember when you were a kid and you were looking forward to your birthday? I certainly do, because I was born in December, and in that month our family also celebrated Christmas and Hanukah. The closer that December got, the slower time seemed to pass; in fact, I was sure that there was some time demon out there deliberately slowing things down for me. Conversely, in the summer, when we had three months of no school, time sped by; that same demon was probably messing with me again.

In other words, as children, the notion of time was relative to the events taking place in our lives: some time went quickly and some, slowly. I also remember as a child thinking that time was something that almost stood still. I had little sense of what "time moving on" meant. At four, I thought I was always four and would always be four. Someone who was forty—as my parents were—had always been a parent. (And by the way, forty was really old.)

The older we get, the faster time passes, and there is very little "relativity"—it all seems to fly by with a blur. It's the adults who say, "I can't believe it's Halloween already." The kids feel they've been waiting an eternity to dress up and get armloads of candy. Why? One reason is that, depending upon our focus, our goals, and what else is happening simultaneously, equal amounts of time—as measured by a stopwatch, a clock, or a calendar—can seem to pass very differently. When we're utterly focused on one thing (as a child often is), time can seem to expand. If you've been in an accident, an earthquake, or put on the spot in a classroom discussion or an interview, you know that just a few seconds can seem to stretch out for long moments.

If Time Is Relative, How Do You Measure It?

It wasn't as dramatic as an accident, an earthquake, or an interview but a slow-moving incident at the Men's Wearhouse that provided me with a new perspective on time. We were making a commercial and trying to fill the time between active work on the shots so that we wouldn't be frustrated by the amount of down time. It was a particularly long, monotonous, and grisly day that drove us to invent a game. By way of background, you should know that for many years, the "team" that made Men's Wearhouse commercials was George, as the owner-spokesman; Jordan, the president of our advertising agency, the producer; and Ivan, the director. I was the referee.

During one of the many breaks in the action, Jordan was bemoaning the lack of "effective" copy in the spot we were shooting. Jordan said: "Ahhh … We never get to really say what we should in a commercial. We shoulda added a lot of things to this spot we're doing, like …" Whereupon, Jordan went on to name a few more selling points that weren't already in the spot.

Ivan took issue, saying: "Wait a minute; this spot is already stuffed like a sausage. You have no idea about the concept of time."

So, more as a way to pass the time than anything else, Ivan came up with a contest to prove his theory about the differing senses of time. He explained the rules, saying, "Okay, while we're sitting here doing nothing else but waiting, I'll start three stopwatches at the same time and say 'go'! We'll each have a chance to shout out when we think thirty seconds are over."

This game sounded interesting, and lacking anything better to do at the moment, I decided we should all play.

With three stopwatches in his hands, Ivan began, "Here goes: ready, set, go … but we have to continue talking now. Jordan, tell us about yourself. Just remember: We're each going to shout out when we think thirty seconds is over."

Ivan asked Jordan a question, then asked one of me; we went back and forth. The questions weren't related to making commercials. They were just general kinds of things. After some time, as Jordan was answering a question, I said "Now." Jordan continued.

After some more time, Ivan said, "Now." Jordan continued … and then he finally said, "Now."

We looked at the stopwatches for the results. I had said, "Now," after seventeen seconds. Only seventeen seconds. I was probably thinking about how much all of the "down time" was costing, and how little we get to say in the short span of thirty seconds. Ivan said, "Now" in exactly thirty seconds, because it was just time, and he had spent a lot of his life timing things like thirty-second increments. Jordan said, "Now," after forty-five seconds, because that's the amount of copy that he *wanted* to put into the thirty-second spot.

It was all about thirty seconds—a sacrosanct number in the advertising business. And there we were, three people—to whom thirty seconds meant a whole lot—with totally different ideas on what thirty seconds actually *was*. None of it was a lot of time, but our sense of it was very different.

For a holiday gift that year, I bought Jordan a stopwatch.

Time Moves On

One final point about time: the older you get, the more you realize how precious time is and how invincible you're not. If you're between twenty and thirty, you're probably rolling your eyes hearing this—yet again—from some old guy. But it's very true and if by noting it here I can help just one person "get it," then it's worth it.

Time in the Balance

Given that time is what you've got, it makes sense to learn how to use it, how to use it well, and how to balance different aspects of your life in relation to it. The following strategies—don't follow the crowd, do one thing at a time (at least sometimes), slow down, meditate, respect timing, and rethink how you spend your time—are designed to help you to get time to work more for you. They're not hard and fast—maybe more like soft and slow. They're easy to do and designed to help you be more efficient with your time—and to not waste it. And, as you'll see, they are all interrelated.

Don't Follow the Crowd

Just because "everyone is doing it" doesn't mean that "it" is the right thing for you. As a teenager, you probably heard something along these lines from a parent or other authority figure who might have also said, "If everyone went out and jumped off a bridge, does that mean you would, as well?" Learn how to find your own path, to find the way that works best for you. It's not the easiest thing to do, and there are risks, but in the end, being the author of your own playbook and rulebook will be the way to go. How do you do this? By learning how to trust yourself, your instincts, your intuition, and your judgment. And how do you learn to do that? By trial and error (again) and with a little assistance from this book.

Here's a very practical example of what I'm talking about. Let's say you're in an airport and see several lines that proceed through the security checkpoint. Or you're at the supermarket and have to choose which of the checkout lines to queue up in. You're in just about any situation where you have to choose which line to enter. Do you go left or do you go right? The answer is, go left. Why? Most people are right-handed, and their entire world is governed by going right. You want to beat the crowd instead of following it? Do what they *aren't* doing. Go left. I wish I could tell you that I had this amazing vision when I figured this out. I didn't. I'm left-handed, and after years of going left, missing the lines, and wondering why, it dawned on me that the reason I missed the lines was because I went left.

The crowd is just that—a crowd. There is no wisdom in numbers— in fact, a crowd's mentality can be downright unwise or even dreadful. Establish your own rules, your own roles, and your own path. If, after doing that, your decision is consistent with the crowd, then so be it.

Do One Thing at a Time (at Least Sometimes)

Remember the five-minute rule? Well, here's a great place to invoke it, because I know that many of you cannot begin to imagine what I now suggest: forget multitasking and learn to do things one at a time. Use the rule and read on—please.

In a phone conversation with my daughter Emily (age thirty-one), I mentioned that one of the points I was going to make in this book was that multitasking isn't a good thing, and that people need to stop doing it. Her response was immediate and unequivocal: "Are you kidding? That's *all* that we do. In fact, while I'm talking to you, I'm also emailing a friend of mine, checking out something online, and listening to music on my computer."

My argument was: Try to learn to pay attention to *one thing*. Computers are meant to multitask, *people aren't*. While it might seem like you're getting more done by doing several things at the same time, most of the time you end up paying much less attention to any *one* of those several things. The effort that you have to exert to re-do something that you weren't paying full attention to the first time around is totally wasted, unproductive, and probably less "in the moment" than it was when it first came up. If you are present—focused on one thing, and then present and focused on the next thing, and then the next thing—you're going to be far more productive than you would have been had you been doing them all at the same time. So do one thing well. Then go out and do the next one thing well. And so on, and so on. It may seem like a risk (that you're losing time, not doing what everyone else is), but try it.

My argument was a retelling of something I felt rather strongly about. Emily's argument was a succinct reminder of the need to keep an open mind and "know that I don't know." In the survey I sent out to the advisory board, 44 percent of the respondents considered themselves "very much" multitaskers, and 31 percent considered themselves "extreme" multitaskers. So I was not surprised that, at a dinner with part of the advisory board, the "need for speed" (not the video game, but the general pace and attitude) kept popping up. As I thought about it, it dawned on me that this was almost part of the DNA of the group. One participant mentioned that theirs was an era of the microwave. There was no need to wait for everyone to have dinner together, because not only was everyone not coming home at the same time, but the defrosting, lengthy roasting, and elaborate cooking were no longer necessary because of the microwave. The microwave could be the symbol of getting things done in the fastest way possible. The discussion of what has been lost in this generational change is for another time, but simply put, it's connectedness.

Some participants at dinner mentioned that one of the advantages of IMs and text messaging is that they get the chance to cut out the BS and get to the point. They said that they rarely leave a voicemail message other than to say, "Call me" and that when hearing a voicemail, if it's more than a sentence, they tune out. Some said that they don't even listen to voicemails, just scan the numbers of missed calls. What can I say? Once again, just because "everyone" is doing it doesn't mean it's a particularly good idea. True, it suits life in a rush, but is it a good use of time? We've all found ourselves in games of telephone tag. And with voicemail and text messaging available, why not give at least the pith of the topic? Assuming your friends and colleagues aren't long-winded, why not listen to the message? If someone took the time to leave it, could be you'll learn something by listening to it—in terms of time, we're only talking about a few seconds.

In fact, we've always multitasked to some degree in our lives (and long before cell phones and other gadgets) but the multitasking usually involved only one piece of technology. (Talking on the phone and washing the dishes, for example.) Technology has allowed us to take it to another level. Since it's now possible to have several technology-based events happen simultaneously, the next logical step might be to *do* them at the same time. Taken separately, these new technologies have produced on the promise of improving the productivity in our lives. The problem is that for some reason, we have decided to use all of these wonderful devices at the same time—whether we're exercising, having coffee (at home or at the local beanery), en route to a meeting, in a meeting, or even on vacation. Fast-moving video games, television programs with multi-visual messages happening at the same time, the ever-present crawl at the bottom of the screen, PDAs, emails, and instant messaging have all created a situation where one rarely has the *chance* to do one thing at a time. But that doesn't negate the benefits of at least *trying* to do one thing at a time.

I've moved away from my former stance on multitasking, which was to offer three words—stop doing it—and then an explanation. Instead, I offer a compromise: Let's not look at this as an "always or never" situation; let's think of it as one of those "in the moment" things. And again, just because "everyone" is doing it doesn't make it right.

Here's one example. How often have you witnessed a driver totally run a red light while talking on the cell phone? That potential consequence is possibly fatal and the message should be clear: using the cell phone while driving has potential for serious trouble; therefore, in *that* moment, it's better to choose one over the other, or at least use your headset or speakerphone and keep both hands on the wheel.

79

Here's another, more subtle example. Let's say a friend wants to share some good news with you, face to face. As a way to show your support for your friend, it might be a good idea for you to turn off your cell phone (or at least turn it to vibrate) and not multitask for that time. Think about the shoe being on the other foot, in different circumstances. This time it's your news, and it's bad news, not good. You have something that's personally really disturbing that you want to share with your friend. You sit down, face-to-face, and begin to talk. Suddenly, his phone rings, and he answers it. Not only does he answer, but as he speaks, you realize that the call is pretty inconsequential. How would you feel?

And here's something in between for you to try as an experiment. The next time you begin a routine task—something you have to do often, like paying bills—try to *not* multitask while doing it. Notice the result. Did you do it faster? With less effort? Did it take less time? The important thing for you to do is to just *try* it—then be the judge.

Maybe children raised today amid technology's latest wonders will become more used to multitasking, but will they be more efficient? Time will tell. In the interim, I can be quite certain that for me, being in the moment and doing one thing at a time will often yield more productive results than doing several things at the same time. Whether it will for you is something for you to determine. Just try the experiment of doing one thing—*any* one thing—without doing something else. Make a concerted effort to stop and decide when multitasking is appropriate and when it isn't. If the supposed point of multitasking is to get more done in less time, the next tip may surprise you even more.

Slow Down

This section is all about getting less done in less time, by learning how to slow down. It's not a typo, and you didn't read it incorrectly; it really is "less done in less time." Moving at a measured pace is one of those things that comes naturally to our bodies. Speeding things up is one of those things we impose on ourselves in an effort to "get more stuff done." Slowing down gives you the chance to notice and appreciate the subtleties in life, to give your senses a chance to do what they're supposed to do—help you become more aware. Slowing down can also help you to find what's meaningful in your life and to help you to find more meaning in those things. The idea of slowing down is really no more than a call to do what comes naturally to your system.

In his novel, *Slowness,* Milan Kundera writes about how we slow down and speed up as relates to our memory. Kundera argues that when a person wants to remember something, he purposely slows down everything else around him in order to concentrate on what he is trying to remember. Conversely, when a person is trying to *forget* something, he speeds up time around himself in order to create distance.

I couldn't help but think back to some of the conversations at the dinner with part of the advisory board. I was still trying to digest the concept of not taking the time to listen to phone messages, of wanting to "cut to the chase and get stuff done." What I thought of as the "need for speed" may as well be part of the air in which many people find themselves today. In fact, much as the idea of speed kept popping up in conversation, many of the twenty- and thirty-year-olds indicated they hadn't been asked to think about speed before—and why should they? They don't see that contemplating the questions and attempting to answer them gets them anywhere. People seem to be in a rush—even if they don't know what they're rushing for or toward. It's "hurry up and get there" and without the "there" being defined. Or, as Yogi Berra said, "If you don't know where you're going, you might not get there." True enough. But when you take a little time to slow down, you'll see more and develop a better sense of your ultimate destination—finding the "there" there.

A good place to begin to slow down is to ask yourself the following question: "What is urgent and what isn't?" This question is "in the moment," meaning that you can answer it only by being calm and being present. It's another example of how the "answers" that you might seek in life are sitting there right inside of you.

Another good question to ask yourself is, "What's the rush to get through something?" Anything that's worth doing is worth doing well or at least with a modicum of intention and attention. Rushing leads to exhaustion, exhaustion leads to carelessness, and carelessness means having to take extra time to correct mistakes or to complete the overlooked details—both resulting in a waste of (you guessed it) *time*.

Finally, be conscious of getting trapped in someone else's speed and pace. It's possible to enter a situation with your own sense of calmness and order and get caught up with external energy and find yourself moving at the speed of the person around you. This can happen without your awareness at a conscious level. What are some clues to tell you that this is happening? Your breathing is the best clue. Are you breathing more rapidly? Is your breathing shallow? Is your pulse rate faster than it normally is? They're all related, and a dramatic change in any one of them is a sign that you're "out of body" at the moment. Again, figuring it out takes awareness, presence, and practice.

Here's a great exercise in slowing down and what can happen when you do. Give yourself time for a long meal by yourself. Make sure it's a meal that doesn't include any caffeinated beverage (coffee, tea, or soda) and that you don't have to rush or watch the clock. Sit down for the meal with no other distractions. Turn off the cell phone, TV, and iPod; put away all reading materials. This is going to be all about you and the food. Sit at the table and eat your meal one bite at a time. After every forkful of food, put your fork down and sit and chew—perhaps even count the chews to yourself—no fewer than twenty times before you swallow. Then pick up your fork again, with another forkful. Try to concentrate on the flavors and smells of the food and the noises that you make while chewing and swallowing.

It may be very difficult to rein in all the little voices, but by focusing on the process of eating, you'll end up slowing down. And if my experience is any indication, you'll find that you eat far less than you normally would. Plus, you'll walk away from the table more relaxed and with a lowered pulse rate. Think about the last meal that you ate. Can you even remember it? What else were you doing when you were eating? Were you just filling up the tank, or were you trying to be a conscious eater? I know that it's not possible to eat consciously all of the time, but doing it every now and then will help you to slow down and also help you to appreciate food.

A terrific resource for the idea of slowing down is *Stopping*, by Dr. David Kundtz. Dr. Kundtz actually differentiates between slowing down and stopping and believes that slowing down doesn't work, per se. I won't split hairs and will agree with Dr. Kundtz that stopping (in my case slowing down) should "precede everything we do as well as assume a position of priority in our lives" (page 31).

MEDITATE

There isn't any way to slow down the passage of time, but there is a way that you can make the minutes and the days *count* more and perhaps be more meaningful. That way is through meditation.

Once again, I'm asking that you employ the five-minute rule. I'm not trying to win you over to an obscure religion or some wacko thought process. I'm trying to get you to think a bit out of the box. Meditation can help you slow down, help create an internal sense of calmness, and help you make better and more informed decisions. While the word *meditation* might conjure up images of incense, beads, or exotic music, try to take a step back and realize that it's just your judgmental voice taking over.

So many people spend so much time trying to get high—I suggest meditation to get low, to get quiet, and to get peaceful. Training your mind to tune out the noises of everything from outside traffic to inside voices is a challenge, but a very worthwhile one.

The cornerstone to meditation is breathing—learning how to control your inhalations and exhalations. Why pay attention to breathing? Think of it like this: what is the *first* thing you do as a being outside of the womb? Breathe. What is the *last* thing that you do as a being outside of the womb? Breathe. It's all the breaths in between (about a billion or so by age fifty) that determine how you are to be in the world. Think about it—if someone told you that you were going to do *one thing* a *billion times* in only part of your life, do you think you would want to pay some attention to it?

There are lots of books and helpful practitioners out there. Two that I recommend are *Wherever You Go, There You Are* by Jon Kabat-Zinn and *The Wooden Bowl* by Clark Strand. And you can try it on your own—now. To begin with, all you need is a floor, a couple of pillows and/or a wall (the pillows and wall are optional and might add to your comfort), and a little patience. Put it together and just sit. Sit and see what happens. Try to sit and be still without attaching any judgment.

Meditation in Ten Easy Steps

1. Find a quiet space.
2. Sit down.
3. Stop thinking.
4. Close your eyes.
5. Stop thinking.
6. Support your back by sitting against a wall, if you need to.
7. Stop thinking.
8. Begin to take slow, deep breaths—inhaling through your nose, then exhaling through your nose. Try to focus all of your attention on just this.
9. Stop thinking.
10. Every time you notice that you are thinking, relax and say, "Just thinking" to yourself.

Those are the basics, but truth be told, it's a little more involved. The hardest thing to do is to quiet all of the little voices that are in your head while you're trying to sit and breathe. While most of the time we don't even realize that the voices are present, they are generally what guide us (for better or for worse) day in and day out. They become especially present and loud when the rest of our being is quiet. Once again, it all takes practice, and once again, it's an example of finding the answers inside of you.

Meditation gives you the ability to be "in the moment"—to see with greater clarity and focus. When you can do this, you can have increased control over situations, can see and implement solutions, and generally approach the world with a greater sense of equanimity. Meditation can also help you to get "out" of the moment, if need be. You might find yourself in a situation that is either tense or uncomfortable—something you have no control over—like a traffic jam. A practice of meditation can give you the ability to not become the traffic and the associated stress, but to simply keep breathing and remain calm. A practice of meditation helps you to focus on the "now" without getting too wrapped up in it. And you need no cool shoes, no colorful bodysuits, and no fancy corkscrews. Yes, it takes time to meditate, but the time you spend in meditation will provide rewards that make it worthwhile, including spending *less* time worrying about things that aren't worth stressing about.

> *It all takes practice. The answers are inside of you.*

And one final point about meditation. Like any other practice, there might be long stretches of time where you just don't do it—for whatever reason. If my experience is any example, after several days, even weeks of not meditating, getting back into it is quite easy. In

86

fact, the first few times that you do it after a hiatus, you might find your "sit" to be especially meaningful.

RESPECT TIMING

There are three aspects to timing: your internal timing, your external timing, and the external timing of others.

Internal Timing (Yours). Your internal body works with its own sense of rhythm and timing. It's a very subtle and real process, so subtle that you are rarely aware of it. But through the process of slowing down, trusting yourself, getting quiet, and trusting your intuition, you can allow your inner body to do what's right for itself in the moment.

I have recently experienced a great example of the importance of knowing my internal timing. While I was working on this part of the book, I underwent some involved knee surgery (a partial knee replacement and ACL reconstruction). I understood that I was going to be out of it mentally for a few days and then spend several days alert, but not getting around much physically. I was looking forward to this time as a chance to get some quality writing done. I was wrong on all fronts. While the good news was that I was awake and alert hours after surgery, it was not the only news. The bad news was that I was mentally out of it for several hours a day for many days after the surgery, thanks to the pain medication that I badly needed. I realized that if I was going to get any serious work done, I'd have to find that short window every day in which I was alert, yet pain free. The process made me much more aware, almost on an hourly basis, of my mental state. The recuperative experience wasn't what I had planned, but by paying attention to my internal timing, I was able to focus when I needed to.

External Timing (Yours). Ego and its function in your life came up in the previous chapter. Here's another way of looking at ego: its goal is to remain on your personal payroll—job assurance, if you will. Procrastinating helps keep your ego working—by encouraging you to resist at all levels. It encourages you to resist change, effort, and anything that might upset your status quo. Think about the things that you procrastinate about. Chances are that many of them have to do with things on your to-do list. Maybe procrastinating about doing your laundry or washing the car comes to mind. They're good small examples, but what about the big ones? Take a look at the larger examples, maybe "holding off" on doing a paper for school or "waiting until later on" to lose weight and get into shape. Bigger yet: not being proactive about changing jobs, if you're not liking your current job.

Procrastinating doesn't get you where you want to be, and it's an enormous waste of time. The amount of energy that you can expend in *not* doing something is often greater than the energy that is needed to do the task to begin with. The psychic energy that you waste in worrying, thinking about the consequences, and second-guessing yourself isn't worth the effort. Put your ego to rest and call up your trust to allow you to move on and stop stalling.

External Timing (with Others). This is simply a fancy way of saying that you should be on time. Be considerate of others' time. If you make a plan to have dinner with a friend at seven, be there at seven.

Being chronically late is not something you inherit; you do have control over it. Try it. Likely you'll find that being considerate of others' time, aside from being the right thing to do (remember: we each have the same number of hours in a day) does actually help you both in the long run.

Rethink How You Spend Your Time

Whether you're a student, employed in the workforce, work out of your home, unemployed, or on vacation, how you spend your time is key and something over which you have more control than you might think. Depending upon your circumstances, some of these tips apply now; some may be useful to you at another time.

Evaluate Your Working Hours. Sure, we've made progress with advances in technology and the advent of telecommuting, but the unfortunate reality is that cell phones, email, and IMs have only made it easier for *more* work. What used to be 9 to 5 has become 24/7. Sit down and create work boundaries. They don't have to be hard and fast—leave room for flexibility and the occasional "emergency" at work. But if a co-worker is calling you at eleven at night to shoot the breeze about office politics or something along those lines, it's a good idea to articulate boundaries with that person. If it's your boss, of course, you may have to handle it differently.

Learn How To Say *No*. One of the greatest time savers in the English language is the little word *no*. The inability to use this word (or fear of using it) leads to overextending oneself, procrastinating on tough projects, and failure to focus on priority tasks. Resist the pressure to perform when you don't think you can do the job right. If you are honest with your employer, chances are you can arrive upon an alternative that makes you both happy.

Look at Your Workspace. If you arrange your work environment in a haphazard and cluttered way, chances are the work that comes out of it is going to be haphazard and cluttered. (Kind of "garbage in, garbage out.") While there is no need to be a neat freak, you can be more productive and waste less time if you are organized.

You can also alter the dynamics of your workspace by doing some simple maneuvering. If you have your own desk in an office, consider *where* your desk is. Can it be moved elsewhere? Sometimes a change of scenery in the room can be energizing. Sometimes, it can also make you more efficient. Move the things on your desk to a different place, to clear the desk and make for a clear surface. Is your phone on the right or the left? Consider this relative to whether you're right-handed or left-handed. It makes a difference when you need to talk and write. Reduce clutter. Is there any reason for piles of papers when those same documents are stored on your computer?

Consider changing the writing materials you work with often. Try something new—new legal pads (they come in different shades), new ink colors, new fonts on your PC—it'll change your whole perspective.

In the overall scheme of things, these are small time savers that can be used to make you more efficient and even more settled in your space. But everything contributes to the whole. On a much larger scale, consider your work in and of itself. If you're working at a job that you don't like, no amount of organizational schemes or furniture rearranging is going to change it. If you're working at a job that you don't like, there is little else that can measure up in terms of wasting your time. Further analysis of the workplace and your place in it is coming in the next chapter. Stay tuned.

What about Free Time? To begin with, forget about the notion of free time. There is no such thing. It's all time, and it all counts. And, as already established, you don't know how much of it you have. Think of free time more like "down" time, which is a necessary part of life. The question is: how much down time do you really need?

Anything you do in your down time is fine. Where many people go astray is how much time they're spending on any one thing. Think of video games. While they're good for hand-eye coordination, fun to play, and a great way to let off steam, playing several hours at a sitting can waste a lot of time. How often do you sit down to do work using the Internet and find yourself aimlessly surfing from one unrelated site to another? It's very easy to get lost, and the next thing you know, your work time has become a lot of down time.

Consider Facebook (and similar social-networking sites) and how much time you spend on it. In an article in the *Washington Post* on December 2, 2007, "Getting to Not Know You," Felipe Schrieberg, a student at the University of St. Andrews in Scotland, explained how he found himself logging in five times a day, reuniting with childhood friends as well as friends of friends of friends—out to people he would neither recognize nor converse with in the real world. Then, finally, during a summer internship, Schrieberg's boss (having viewed *his* profile) unnerved him when he commented on Schrieberg's personal status and movie preferences. Schrieberg reassessed how much information he'd provide on Facebook, stopped updating it and checking it incessantly, and discovered he had a lot more time—time he's since used to meet people face-to-face.

You'll have to self-monitor how you spend your time. A good place to start is to designate the time and the duration of down time and stick to those limits. It's called practicing discipline. Remember that all we have is time—and, it seems, there's not enough of it. So use it well.

Here's one final idea about remembering to have time work for you. The next time someone asks you what time it is, try saying (probably to yourself), "It's now."

When Time Is Up

One day, your time will be over. You're not immortal. You don't have all the time in the world. What do you want to leave behind? Have you thought about your legacy? Have you thought about what endures? What is your passion? Have you thought about what exactly you are going to give back? These are all good questions to consider *now*, because you can start doing something about your legacy *today*. A meaningful, lasting legacy may take many forms—children, grandchildren, a business, an idea, a book, a home ... some piece of yourself. It doesn't have to be money or even require money. It can be your time, your experience, or your knowledge. At its core, a real legacy is that piece of yourself that makes

> *You're not immortal. You don't have all the time in the world.*

a difference in the big puzzle of the universe. We all have a piece to contribute. It's up to us to fashion it and put it into place. In order to have the legacy, you have to be conscious of your behavior, your time, and your goals. Now is the time to think about your legacy. It may be a big piece or a small piece—and each piece matters.

Lesson Learned: Legacies

My Aunt Ethel left me a number of legacies. It turns out that in addition to teaching me to try, not to succumb to mental blocks, and assume that I couldn't do something (the story of getting me to paint, as mentioned in chapter 2, is just one example), my Aunt Ethel also taught me about the value of time—my time and other people's. And in the process, she also taught me about confidence and not selling yourself short.

When I graduated from college, I had no idea what I wanted to do, so I moved home to sort out my possibilities. I went to work at Boston Hardware, the family's store. The second floor of the store was mostly my domain—the carpet department. Customers would choose what they wanted from the large rolls of discontinued or irregular carpets, we'd cut the appropriate amount off of the roll, and that was it. But the real money maker for the second floor—and for the entire store—was my Aunt Ethel's interior design business. In her small second-floor studio, she generated nearly half the store's income and considerably more than half of the profits.

Ethel was bright, brash, and afraid of nothing. She was talented and not at all shy about it. She decorated the finest homes in the area and beyond—including homes in New Jersey and Manhattan. Her clients would schlep for hours to come to Hazleton for her advice and expertise. Often, Ethel would confer with me for carpeting questions and advice, more for show for her customers than to acquire any real knowledge. When she did, she introduced me as her resident "expert" in floor covering.

One day she came to me to inquire about a particular roll of carpeting that was in stock and selling for $9.95/yard. (Keep in mind that this was 1973.) She needed carpeting for the playroom of one of her customers, and she wanted to know if there was enough on the roll for her use. There was, and she asked me to set it aside and write up a bill of sale for her client—at $15/yard. It was a huge markup. I was appalled. "How can you sell this to your client for that price, knowing that they could walk back here by themselves and buy it for less?" I asked.

Her answer was short and to the point. "Because they are buying it from *me*, not you," she answered. She went on to explain that the store was entitled to the extra income because of her expertise (and of course implying that in buying it from me, they *weren't* getting the same expertise). Part of what her customers were buying was her vast knowledge and experience, and their time savings. "Your knowledge is worth something. Never sell yourself short," she said. Her voice, and her advice, have stayed with me ever since.

There's also an important legacy that my father, Aaron Goldman, provided to me. He was from a generation of men who naturally picked up where *their* fathers had left off. His father, my grandfather,

Sam Goldman, had opened the first Boston Hardware store in West Hazleton, Pennsylvania, in 1912, and his second store in Hazleton a few years later. (It would seem that the multi-store gene is in my DNA.)

The stock market crashed in 1929, followed by the Great Depression. Consumer demand from 1929 to 1941 was low, and factories making consumer goods scaled back on their capacities, creating short supplies of practically everything. In 1939, a year after he graduated from Rutgers, my dad returned to Hazleton to help out at Boston Hardware, which was struggling to stay afloat. By all accounts, the best plan then would have been to declare bankruptcy, but my dad wouldn't allow it. Instead, he worked with the suppliers of the store to continue to ship merchandise, but by 1941, that struggle became almost secondary as the U.S. entered World War II, placing even *more* demand on supplies of practically all consumer goods and the materials needed to make them. The resulting pressure on retail stores, such as Boston Hardware, was crushing.

In 1942, my dad enlisted in the Army and made an unheard of deal with all of the suppliers (somewhere between forty and fifty companies). He devised a fifty-month deferred payment plan— paying everyone 2 percent each month of the balance owed them. The transaction was accomplished with no attorneys, just with a lot of promises. My dad ended up "minding the store" while he was off in Europe, fighting the war. His choices in all of this mess? Just this: he chose to enlist (the alternative was being drafted), and he chose to pay the suppliers. He had his own dream, which was not Boston Hardware, but continued the family business through difficult times, war, and military service. It could not have been easy for Dad, but it was a given.

Having not had—or not felt he had—a choice, my father's legacy to me was choice. While there was certainly a lot to be said about the family business and the legacy that I might have inherited, the real legacy for me was not the business per se; it was the clear message that my father constantly gave me about choices. The message was that I had a choice—I could choose the business, or I could choose anything and everything else. How did I know this? He simply stated this option repeatedly. Dad had no choice, and he made sure that all three of his children knew that they did. And while none of us chose to remain in Hazleton and take over the store, there is no way that any of us could have (or would have) even attempted to live our dreams if it weren't for this precious legacy that he gave us: choice and thus the time to pursue our own dreams. And, having been raised in business, we all knew there was work ahead, whatever our dreams entailed.

5

You Are Going
to Have to Work

OVER THE COURSE OF YOUR life, the one thing that you're going to do that will take up most of your time and much of your energy and that, in the long run, will be what ultimately defines who you are is the work that you do. It is also a large part of the meaning of your life. It is the way in which you can draw out and exercise your unique qualities in order to expand your consciousness and in order to leave your mark on the world. Whether you work for yourself or are part of a company with thousands of workers, work is the portal to the rest of your life.

And while it is often not referred to as work, parenting definitely falls in this category. It is, without a doubt, the most difficult work that there is. It is a "job" that requires extraordinarily long hours, pays no money (in fact, requires your money, constantly), grabs at your soul like nothing else you'll ever experience, and that, in the long run, will be the most rewarding job you ever have.

If you have chosen to be a stay-at-home parent and can make this happen in your life, I applaud you. There is nothing—nothing—that will ever come close to the meaning, importance, and satisfaction you will get out of being a parent. Unfortunately, because of a bit of misadvertising and a bit of misogyny, in many circles, "just" being a parent does not carry a lot of status. How often do you meet someone and one of the first questions you or they ask is, "What do you do?" If the response is, "I'm a stay at home parent," or something along those lines, too often the reaction is often a murmured, "Oh" followed by the next question, "What did you do before you were a parent?" as if the *now* of being a parent is meaningless. Far from it.

If being a stay-at-home parent is what you have chosen to do, wear that decision with pride. Your child has no idea how lucky (and I *do* mean lucky) he or she is. And the next time you're asked what you do, answer that question with pride, as well. If you get a dismissive, "Oh" in response, remember that the answer is more a reflection of the other person than a statement about you. And if you're so inclined, you might want to mention that if you do what you are doing effectively, you'll change a generation. The rest of this chapter might not appear to apply directly to you as a stay-at-home parent, but there are important lessons for you nonetheless. And one day, once your child is either in school or in some way less needful of you, there will be the rest of the working world waiting out there for you, whether you join in as a paid employee or in some volunteer capacity. This chapter will help you along those lines as well.

For now, whatever your role today, take a few moments to consider a Zen story that has taken many forms and been retold through the years; this version is drawn from *Soul Prints: Your Path to Fulfillment*, by Marc Gafni:

> A Zen master enters a village and sees people scurrying about. "Where are you running?" he asks. "To make a living," they respond. "Why are you so sure that your living is in front of you?" he probes. "Maybe it's behind you and can't catch up. Do not run to make a living, be still and live." (page 35)

Living and Working with Purpose

Everything that arises in your life is there for one purpose only—to teach you to exercise an underutilized aspect of your life. Because work involves contact with other people, the underutilized aspects of your life can become more apparent as you compare and contrast yourself with others. Of course, this can only happen when you're present. Sometimes this can be particularly painful; it's a natural reaction to resist and avoid those aspects of ourselves that are weak. But sometimes the most painful lessons are the ones that have the most benefit in the long run.

First, there has to be a you, and then there is your job. Similarly, as a parent, although you are responsible for the development of your child, you are still you. The previous chapters have helped you look at that being who is you; this chapter takes it one step further in helping bring that inner self to the workplace. The most important aspect in doing that is congruency—striving to match your inner self with your outer self and creating harmony between your heart and your head. When we look at the outer world, we don't see the world as it is; we see it only as we are at that moment. Yes, you're going to have to work, but if you can see that when you change your beliefs, you change the world around you, the chances of your creating congruency increase exponentially.

Here's a simple way to think about changing your beliefs and how doing so changes the world around you. Have you ever bought a car and then suddenly noticed how many cars the same as the model you bought are on the road? It's a pretty common reaction. But there aren't really any more of those cars on the road (except yours): what has changed is your awareness of that particular make and model of car. By purchasing the car that you did, you changed your vested interest in the car, and you brought a new level of attention to it, thereby changing your view and belief about that car.

The discussion of work in this chapter is divided into seven sections:

1. Why work?
2. What are you "supposed" to do?
3. What are you doing?
4. You are going to have to struggle.
5. You are going to have to develop discipline.
6. Success isn't easy or self-sustainable.
7. Are you going to be the CEO?

These sections cover work from the inside (how do *you* approach work) to the outside (what does your *work* have to do with you).

Why Work?

When you sit down and think about your life, think about this: the question is not what or why, but *how* are you going to live? Work is an integral part of how you're going to live and how you are going to be in the world. A fulfilling life is passion driven and a big part of that life derives from the work that you do. It doesn't matter *what* the work is. What matters is the passion that you have behind it and that you put into it. The same applies for the rest of your life.

Each one of us has a reason for being and a contribution to make; why not strive to make these more than financial survival? Yes, finances are important, but if you work at a job that just pays the bills without providing an outlet for your passion, then the ultimate cost to you is far more than the bills that might be due. The cost is compromising and stifling your creative intellect and wasting your time—a whole lot of it. Know that you can be in control, at the helm of your own destiny, by the decisions you make in all aspects of your life—especially regarding the work that you choose to do and how you choose to do it. Remember that everything counts: you will be at your happiest when you are expressing your essential nature and creating your mark on the world through the work that you do.

Do you always seem to have a "bad boss" or "never get a break" at work? It may have something to do with what *you* are presenting to the world. Your outer working life has to reflect your inner organization. Make sure that you have your personal values and ethos in order, and then take them to the workplace. The reality is that there are no bad bosses, and there are no bad breaks. And there are no victims—unless you choose to become one. ***Stop!*** Take a moment to re-read this paragraph. It's easy enough to read, but really understanding the content can take a lifetime. Give yourself an advantage and contemplate it now: what you bring to your work makes all the difference.

> *There are no bad bosses, and there are no bad breaks.*

What Are You Supposed to Do?

Each of us has our own specific "true calling"—an answer to the question, "What am I supposed to do?" At the most fundamental level, we each need to feel like we are doing something worthwhile and that we are making a positive contribution to the planet. We need to be able to leave work at the end of the day, feeling tired yet energized because we've done something that matters and that our work outside the home has meaning.

How do you figure out who you are, what your place in the world is, and what you're "supposed" to do? If you grew up in a supportive family, you were told that you could be anything you set your mind to. That's a lovely message, but it's pretty nonspecific. If you grew up in a household with less support, non-specificity is the least of your problems.

Figuring out what you're supposed to do is actually simpler than you think: *do what brings you joy.* **Stop!** Think about that right now. If there were no negative consequences—financial or otherwise—what do you see yourself doing for work that would bring you joy? Is it possible for you to be doing that "thing" at this moment in your life? Perhaps not, but you've taken one important step in getting to that "thing" by identifying it to begin with. You can begin the process of getting there *right now.*

Is it easier said than done? Sure, but if you pay attention, your intuition will guide you. Sometimes it's tricky to differentiate between the voice of your ego and the voice of your soul. The voice of your ego is the one that tells you what you "should" be doing, based mostly on voices and opinions that you have heard and continue to hear from the outside world. This is *not* a helpful voice. The voice of the soul is the one that will keep gently drawing you to the things you love. When you follow your heart's desire and listen to your intuition, work turns into pleasure. Will it always be this way? Probably not, which is why paying attention—being present, quiet, and calm—is also imperative in your work life. What you're sure you should be doing at this stage of your life might end up being what you need to be getting away from five years from now. Times change, and people change. Getting quiet not only helps you find your *self,* it also helps you find your right *place for the right time,* by trusting your own inner voice.

What Are You Doing?

As you're contemplating what you're supposed to be doing, also ask yourself this question: "What am I doing with my life now?" It is certainly a pretty big question, and it's one that you have to pause and ask yourself often. Time, that old enemy, is moving on, and if you don't stop and ask the really tough questions, you'll find yourself very old and very upset that you've spent your time doing "work" that you didn't want to do.

When was the last time you woke up in the morning and were really *excited* about the work that you're about to do? Take a moment to really think about that question. Was it this morning? Yesterday morning? Maybe it wasn't even last week or last month. If it was last year, then it's past time to take a hard look at what you're doing. And read on.

If the work that you do is diminishing your ability to live an abundant life rather than adding to it, it is time to make a change. By identifying your unique skills and talents, you can discover the true meaning in your life and live more authentically. You won't be able to do this if your work is taking from, rather than adding to, your life.

If you're currently employed and wondering about why you're there, ask yourself the following questions:

- Is the work inspirational as well as perspirational?
- Are you inspiring others?
- Are you leaving others in a better condition than you found them?
- Are there people in the company that you admire?
- Do you admire the company?
- If you weren't working there and it was possible to avail yourself of your company's product or service, would you?
- Is the work complementary to the rest of your life?
- Is it using your abilities to develop greater capacities?
- Is there a place for your beliefs and values?
- Are your little idiosyncrasies welcomed, tolerated, or outright shunned?
- Does it just plain feel right?

If your answer to most of these questions is no, then you need to take a long, hard look at what you're doing. First, make your best effort to change your own position, and even take a stab at improving the culture around you. If you feel that you've done this to no avail, you need to develop your exit plan. I'm not advocating that you turn in your resignation tomorrow—there are bills to be paid and responsibilities to be met—but for your own well-being, you need to begin to work in the direction of leaving your current work and finding something else that has more meaning for you.

If you are a student in college or graduate school and you feel that you're in a rut or have answered *no* to many of the above questions, then you need to reevaluate your situation. Again, start from a place of changing the current situation—don't let "bail" be the default answer. Maybe the *no* answers have to do with what you're doing when you're not in class, or not studying. You're the best judge.

A degree is important, but if it comes at the cost of boredom, then it's an expensive lesson, both financially and spiritually. Perhaps you've chosen the wrong major; know that it's never too late to right that wrong. Perhaps you're trying too hard to graduate in X number of years and have overloaded yourself with courses; that decision is another wrong that can be righted. Maybe you're just burned out with school. Most colleges make it pretty easy for you to either take a leave of absence or to cut back on your course load. Take advantage of that flexibility in any way you can.

If you're a parent who feels like you have stayed at home too long, you have choices as well. How old are your children? Do they need you 24/7 or is there a way that you can get out of the house during part of the day to do something that challenges your intellect a little more? For that matter, given the wide range of possibilities on the Internet, you can take a course, start a business, or be involved in something greater than yourself from your home at any hour of the day—even at sporadic naptimes. You just have to make the commitment to do it.

The question, "What am I doing?" is not a question that you can ask yourself once in life and then be done. It is a question that you should ask yourself often—maybe daily. It's far too easy to get stuck in a situation where you are comfortable, where asking *any* question, especially, "What am I doing?" involves way too much risk. Well, know this: the risk, the penalty, for *not* asking the question often enough is far greater than the reward for ignoring the question. If work is indeed the portal to the rest of your life, and the way you can bring out your unique qualities, then you need to ask the questions to ensure that you are being and doing the best that you can. If a path feels like a struggle, is part of the struggle because it's not the right path for you? This is not to say that the path will be easy, but if the obstacles come from within, they may be telling you something you need to pay attention to.

And finally, one of the ways to find out what you "should" be doing is to discover what you *shouldn't* be doing. I suppose this is code for *get a job*! One way to find out what you like is to discover what you don't like, so don't be dismissive of jobs that you don't *think* you're going to like. And be careful of becoming a "professional student." Several members of my advisory board indicated that they were going to school because they hadn't figured out what they wanted to do with their lives. An undergraduate degree is important, but unless you know what you want to do with a degree beyond that, be careful. School is very expensive and very time-consuming; some breathing room and exposure to the working world after so many years in school is probably a good thing.

You Are Going to Have to Struggle

Somewhere along the line, whether you're taking required college courses, applying for a job, looking for a raise, or contemplating leaving a job, you're going to have to struggle with some issues and strive for your goals. No matter what the job, no matter what the circumstance, *you* are going to have to be your biggest advocate. The reason is simple: no one knows you better, and no one is going to look after your own interests better than you. The struggle doesn't have to mean anger, hostility, or fisticuffs. It can mean taking your stand, making your argument, and then listening to the other side. One way or another, these will be defining moments because they will make you look to your values to decide what's worth the struggle, if it's a battle for you, and how to live with the resolution.

Is the Issue Worth the Struggle?

Choose your moment, and choose your fight. There is never any shortage of issues that arise. You have to decide what is worth fighting for and when. How do you do that? To begin with, you decide by being calm and not overreacting to a stressful situation. Your lessons in practicing presence will help. You will also have to develop a sense for looking at the other side. In order to conduct a reasonable fight, you have to be able to get out of your own shoes and get out of your own way and understand what the other side is thinking. Your new habit of reading conflicting points of view (recommended back in chapter 2) will help. Remember that no matter how passionate you are about your side and your beliefs, there are others out there who are equally passionate about *their* beliefs. Understanding this will not only make you better at arguing your point of view, but it will also make you better at being compassionate, as opposed to merely passionate.

Is It Your Battle?

The comments about integrity in chapter 3, "Everything Counts," also apply to fighting. No fight is worth compromising your integrity, and no fight is worth risking the chance of permanent scars, either literal or figurative. You can always agree to disagree agreeably. Doing so requires discipline and a sense of maturity on both sides. You have control over your part. You might have to model some different behavior to make your point to the person on the other side. Keep in mind, though, that you don't have to win all of the battles, and some you should and can sit out entirely.

Can You Live with the Resolution?

At some point, there will be some sort of resolution. Can you be flexible? Sure, you can see your side, but how well have you seen the other side? Are you willing to compromise? Are you willing to move on, regardless of the outcome, and without holding a grudge? Holding your ground means sticking to what you believe in; and this shouldn't preclude new learning. Be willing to change your mind as circumstances and the world around you change. The ground moves sometimes; so should you. These are all situations for which only you have the answer, and that answer can only be dealt with in the moment—in that time that you're in conflict with someone else.

When resolving an issue, trace the history of the dispute and put yourself in the other person's shoes. Resolution is not about settling the score or getting even. Instead, resolution is about doing what's right and comfortable—and forget about getting even.

You Are Going to Have to Develop Discipline

Not doing something may very often seem to be the easiest way. You get a phone call from someone and you either don't know the person or you know it's someone don't want to talk to. What's easy way out? Ignore the call. You get a document or proposal to review, but you just don't have the energy to review it. So you approve it with nothing more than a cursory glance. You wake up in the morning and just don't feel like going to work. You go, but without first making the effort to get in the proper frame of mind. As a consequence, you are so unproductive that your co-workers might have been better off without you that day.

The hard work is always in the present. The day you think the hard work is in the past is the day there is no future. You have to develop the discipline to work and to work hard, no matter what the circumstances. And you're going to have to develop the discipline inside what you're doing to stay focused and not let yourself be swayed by the "shiny object" or get lost on meaningless work. This personal discipline has to then be directed toward your career, to keep you focused on what it is that you want to accomplish and what you're willing to sacrifice in order to make that happen.

Success Isn't Easy, and It's Not Self-Sustainable

Decide right now that you're going to be successful, and decide right now that you're going to be able to handle that success when the time comes. "Ha!" you might say—"I should be so lucky! I'll cross that bridge when I get to it." If you want to design your own luck and put yourself on the path to success, start planning for it now. The graveyard of successful people who didn't know how to handle their success is full. There's no need for you to join them.

What really is success? Maybe a good place to start is to articulate what success *isn't*. It's not a big house, a fancy car, or a bunch of bling. It's not the American Express platinum card or the limousine. Success isn't easy, and once you have it, there is no guarantee that you'll keep it. So prepare for success by accepting that success does not equal significance or security. Success is, quite simply, peace. Peace of mind that you've done the best that you can. Peace of heart that you are part of something—perhaps a family—whose members support you, love you, and will always be there for you.

> *Success does not equal significance or security.*

What might success look like? Is it giving your all? Is it doing your best? Is it getting the job done? Again, it's none of the above. Success is much more about the journey than the end of the road. It's about the experience of your passion. It's the satisfaction you can get from planning and then doing, and then watching the seeds of your planning and doing take root and create something that wasn't there before. Real success is the ability to embrace the discoveries and enlightenment you encounter along the journey in whatever it is that you do. Crossing the finish line is inconsequential. Or, as late singer Harry Chapin once wrote, "It's got to be the going, not the getting there that's good." You will never arrive; you're always, and only, just "here."

Who defines success? We all measure success differently. The best measure and the only one that really counts is how *you* define it. Before beginning a project, decide what *you* think a successful outcome might look like. Use that as your barometer—nothing else.

Then, what are you going to do once you're successful? Once you've done *well,* redouble your efforts to do *good.* Once you've become successful, you might have the money to give some back. You'll certainly have the expertise, so part of what you can give back is the knowledge that you've gained on the way to being successful.

At any point on the trail to success, and at many points after, there is always the temptation to take the easy way out. If you've achieved some success, chances are you already know that there aren't any shortcuts. But once you've achieved this success, you have to remind yourself of how you got there in the first place; surely it wasn't a single-handed effort. Remember to thank, appreciate, and reward the people who have helped you along the way. Have the self-discipline to do the right thing, rather than the easy thing, and hopefully integrity will intersect the two.

With success comes privilege. While I would love to contest that, it's a reality that is far bigger than I am. It's important to keep in mind that the greater our privilege, the greater our obligation to avoid acting special—more importantly, to avoid even *feeling* special.

111

If you're successful, then good for you! But just let it end at that. And move on. Nobody's *that* special.

Sometimes the road up the corporate ladder can be so consuming that you miss your original goal. You push and push to get that next raise, that next promotion, and one day you turn around and you've lost touch with yourself—and in many cases, you've lost touch with your family. You don't *always* need the next toy, that bigger house, or that office with the big window and great view. None of it is worth it if in the process you lose sight of who you are or lose your connection with the people most important to you. All of that is a danger if you subscribe to the theory that success equals money.

Are You Going to Be the CEO?

Just as money doesn't buy happiness, if you think being the CEO will bring you happiness, there's another bubble to burst. If you've envisioned yourself as the Big Kahuna, don't bet the farm. So many people want (or at least *think* that they want) to lead. But the numbers are against them. By definition, there is only one captain, one quarterback, or one CEO and a limited number of teams and companies. Given that, what do you do? Realize that there are leaders and there are followers. For the vast majority, the question is, how can you be a good follower and still have that role be consistent with the rest of your life? How can it be consistent with your values and your dreams? A great way to start is to attach significance before you attach meaning: be absolutely clear about what your objective is when you're getting into a job. If your values and your dreams are more important to you than a title, then it should be pretty easy to accept that you're not going to be the CEO.

It also helps to know a little about group dynamics. Whether it's a class, a fraternity, a club, a company, or a nonprofit, whenever you get a group of people organized under one name or entity, group dynamics are critical. In any group, the work that you do is an exchange between you and the group. It is an exchange of ideas, values, time, effort, energy, and sometimes money. The difference between successful and unsuccessful groups is the ability to keep that exchange open and productive. If people are free to ask questions and know what they can expect from each other, they are more inclined to be productive and content in their roles, to trust one another, and to want to share in a commitment to a common vision.

In any group, people will sift out to a leader, an additional person or two who lead in certain areas, some willing followers, and some followers who are less than willing, to say the least. If most people become followers, how do you become a great follower? To begin with, you have to learn to shelve your ego. There will always be times that you think you know more or can do more than the leader. What do you do then? You learn to make your point, state your opinion, and *move on.*

Some other tips on not only living with but also *being* a great follower:

- Recognize that being a follower is not a failure—it's a function. It's a necessary function, just as any and every other part of a team.
- One day, you are going to be *a* leader, just not *the* leader. (See chapter 6.)

113

- Within any organization, opportunities exist for any one person, regardless of rank, status, or title, to shine.

- Oftentimes being a follower means acting like you're the leader when faced with any and everything that you do. If it's your project, then you're the leader.

- You can be a follower without abdicating your self. In fact, being a follower can help you in defining your self—it's a terrific lesson in learning how to put your ego in neutral.

In thinking about being a follower or a leader, consider that it may be a matter of perspective. Are you looking up the ladder to see who's above, are you looking at the rung you're on to see who else is there, or are you looking at the rung below? Instead of worrying where everyone else is, try to reconcile yourself with the possibility that you are in the right place, making the absolute best of the resources you have available to you *on that day*.

Lesson Learned: Work, not *Rachmunus*

For several years, I was the person who planned out the buy for suits, sport coats, and slacks; went out and bought them; scheduled the deliveries; decided what merchandise was going to what stores; and finally, presented the buys to our employees in the stores. Needless to say, it was an intense job, but it kept me close to the merchandise and close to the stores. I always believed that figuring out why something was selling was easy; the hard part was trying to figure out why something was *not* selling. To know why products weren't selling, I needed to stay close to the stores, and talk to the people who were dealing with customers on a daily basis.

There was a particular manufacturer (not the Stinky Suits vendor) from whom we bought many suits. This vendor's suits were some of those that just didn't sell well—year after year. After speaking to the employees, I found out that the biggest problem was the inconsistency in the manufacturing of the product: sometimes the suits fit well, and other times, they fit poorly. Sometimes the fabrics were great, other times, poor. The sales force had basically lost confidence in the product, thus not showing it to customers, resulting, of course, in poor sales. I had told the president of the company on several occasions that the suits were not selling well. He was a good friend, with whom I often shared more than business reflections, so when I had to inform him that we weren't going to buy any more suits from his company, he wasn't entirely surprised.

That night over dinner, he acknowledged that he was also concerned about the problems that I had discussed, and he told me that he was considering leaving the company because of his frustration and because he felt like he wasn't being heard. He had an offer from another company and wanted to know my opinion about leaving. The owner of the company he was working for was a very tough man, and I could only imagine his frustration in working for him. I thought the job change was a good idea and told him as much.

A few months later, my friend became president of the other company. He called and asked me to see him on my next trip to New York. I did and looked at his clothing and found that it wasn't really a good fit for Men's Wearhouse. Why? I had an issue with the quality and the price. He countered by suggesting that I buy something as a good-will gesture to him—the Yiddish word he used was "rachmunus."

I told him that our friendship was one thing and that our business relationship was another. I went on to explain that when I bought suits for Men's Wearhouse, I was putting my reputation and the reputation of the company on the line. My reputation was at stake because I knew that I had to "sell" the suits to the store managers in order to get them behind the product. The reputation of the company was at stake because the managers and the sales people had to sell the suits to actual customers. I went on to explain that when a Men's Wearhouse store manager wanted to know why we were now carrying that particular suit, I didn't think "rachmunus" was going to be an acceptable explanation for the manager *or* the customer.

What happened to our relationship? There is bad news and good news. The bad news is that we didn't speak to each other much for a few years, and when we did, the communication was tense and short. The good news is that time—as is so often the case—heals all wounds. After a few years, and after the suits by his new company had greatly improved in quality, we became friends once again, and Men's Wearhouse began to sell the suits. And after a drink or two at an apparel show, my friend looked at me, winked, and said, "You were right. Thanks." I wasn't sure what I was "right" about, but having my friend back meant more to me than knowing that particular answer.

It's clear that the work part of your life is going to take center stage. And once that you've entered that arena, the next hurdle is management—both management of yourself and yourself as a manager. After all, one day, somehow, some way, you will be called upon to manage. There is no time like the present to start preparing, as you'll see in the next chapter.

6

Manage Yourself First; Then Manage Others

THIS CHAPTER IS ABOUT MANAGEMENT: first, learning how to manage yourself, and then managing others. Self-management begins by knowing yourself from the inside out—an idea broached in the first few chapters of this book. And there's more. Self-management is about self-discipline—learning to know the difference between impulse and desire. It's also about establishing priorities—and having the discipline to stick with those priorities.

This chapter is also about taking control of your work life, whether it's while you're in school or once you enter the workplace. Yes, as I pointed out in the last chapter, you're probably not going to be the CEO—few people are. However, you are already *a* CEO—of yourself. So first, make sure you manage yourself well, and then look to managing (otherwise known as leading) others.

Managing Yourself First

To help you learn to manage yourself, I offer a set of don'ts: habits and traits to watch. If you find them in yourself, learn to take control of them, and make sure that you manage to best advantage. Conquer these don'ts with the recommendations given here and you'll be a better person, a better manager, and a better leader.

DON'T WAIT FOR SOMEONE ELSE TO TEACH YOU

Practically whatever the task, if you teach it to yourself, you'll learn it better. The easy way out is to have someone sit down and parse information to you, kind of how toddlers are fed before they learn to manage using spoons on their own. The harder way is to go out and figure it out by yourself. This might require a bit of research on your part; you may need to end up asking a bunch of questions. It may be time consuming—and it's the right way to go. Just keep in mind that the only "stupid" question is the one that you don't ask.

When you're done asking and researching and when you've figured out something new, whatever it is, the next thing that you have to do is to share the knowledge—pass it along. Learn to be a mentor and to be helpful in having the next person gain the knowledge.

DON'T WAIT FOR SOMEONE ELSE TO GIVE YOU A CHOICE; CHOOSE FOR YOURSELF

If you have to wait for someone else to make choices for you, in all likelihood, you'll have poor ones to choose from. If you're unsure about your choices, make the best possible choice given the information you have in front of you. Whether the decision is right or wrong, making your own decision will still be better than letting someone else make the decision for you. It's part of the process of learning.

Don't Settle For Less; Follow Your Dreams

Every dreamer pays a price, but so does everyone who fears to dream. The price for not dreaming or ignoring dreams is much higher. Every now and then, sit down and let yourself imagine. Let your mind go, and let all of the inner voices have a rest. Think about what the world might look like if your contribution to it was unfettered, if it was pure and simple and unbiased. Daydreaming is an important part of your creative process; allow yourself to do it often. It is the way to open your heart and to shut down your head. There is nothing to lose and everything to gain. Your head has all the "what ifs"— the obstacles, the speed bumps, and the warning signs. And yes, it's important to be conscious and present, with your eyes open and in protective mode most of the time. But it's equally important to do the exact opposite: to let go and put no limits on yourself. After all, it's only a daydream.

Here's a good way to encourage yourself to daydream: every day, spend at least five minutes looking at something that's several miles away, or even better, looking into infinity. Most of our day is spent looking at objects that are merely a few feet in front of us—like computer screens and cell phones. For many of us, the farthest that we might be looking over the course of the day is the distance that we look while we're driving. You don't have to live in the mountains or on the beach in order to look out at nothing—sit back and look at the sky. Let your eyes focus on nothing; it will help open your mind to doing the same. After your mind has done this, daydreaming becomes much easier.

DON'T SELL YOURSELF SHORT—EVER

Don't doubt your abilities, and don't doubt your talents. Forget about what you've been led to believe by the media or people in your life. That's a journey that's not productive. As the American psychologist Abraham Maslow once said, "Learn to become independent of the good opinion of other people." Recognize your strengths, and listen to your inner voice; believe your inner voice over the voice of advertising or of others. Eliminate "I can't" from your personal lexicon.

DON'T ACCEPT OR EXPECT MEDIOCRITY

Expect excellence of yourself to begin with; then, with others. The minute you expect less of yourself is the same minute that your inner self will get the compromised message and start delivering less. Push yourself—always.

Push others, as well, in a gentle, affirming way. Push yourself as a consumer out in the marketplace. Let's say you walk into a fast-food restaurant. You're probably hungry and not expecting a lot. Does that mean you have to put up with something less than courteous service, a clean environment, and a warm meal? Absolutely not. As a consumer, you are entitled to great service wherever you go, and when you don't get it, speak up! The people running any business you frequent can't be at every location every day, and they can't always see what's going on, so they really want and need constructive feedback.

Don't Worry about Being the Best

Believe it or not, you just have to be better than the people around you. Do you think that Men's Wearhouse assembled the smartest and the best retailers on the planet? Not quite. The company *did* assemble the people who demonstrated the want and the desire to succeed. And the company did everything *just a little better* than the competition. There's a wonderful joke that relates to this:

Two men were walking through the forest when in the distance they saw a bear approaching them. The first man started to run away. The second man stopped and put on his running shoes. In disbelief, the first man called, "What are you doing? The bear is running after us!" The second man answered calmly, "I don't have to outrun the bear; I only need to outrun you."

Just learn to outrun everyone else. Instead of trying to be the absolute best, strive to be the best that you can be at that particular function on that particular day. It's the experience of trying that really counts.

Worrying about being the best can also prevent you from even *trying* new things or taking on new responsibilities. Let new things just be that—new—with no personal judgment attached and no preconceived notions of how they're going to proceed or work out and with no worries about how you might look.

Don't Ask for a Favor; Bring an Opportunity

A long time ago, my gut told me not to accept Bob Day's opinion that I wasn't ready to be hired by his advertising agency. In a nanosecond after hearing him say, "No," I was able to come up with a "yes" scenario and an opportunity that cost him nothing and ultimately helped both of us. The next time that a problem comes up, stop and look at it and let yourself contemplate the first solution that comes to mind—no matter how crazy. The worst thing that's going to happen is that you'll ultimately decide against it. Learn to look at problems as opportunities for learning and for expanding your universe.

Don't Hide Your Strengths; Develop Them and Use Them Well

You undoubtedly have some aptitudes you were born with and more that you've developed. Use them all. Develop your confidence in them and in yourself. Know your weaknesses, and use your strengths to overcome them.

Why do many of the most successful people succeed? Confidence. Learn how to *act* confident, even when you might not *feel* confident. Confidence is the result of the most important relationship you will ever have: the relationship with yourself. Like all relationships, it begins with trust. The ability to trust yourself draws out of you an emotional power that reflects outward as self-assurance. Being confident is reflected in the expression of your creative abilities and is demonstrated in your power to create. Confident people are in control of themselves, exude composure, and are emotionally secure relative to trusting their own ideas. One of the many tests of true confidence is the ability to stand in your truth against all odds. When you know something is right while everyone else is saying "No! No! No!"—that's confidence. Your self assurance, coming from the trusted place within you—deep down inside—is your truth. You will be tested many times.

> *Know that your confidence will illuminate the path to the next step.*

Remember: if you know *why* you feel very confident about your idea, decision, or direction, even if the solution is not *yet* visible, know that your confidence will illuminate the path to the next step.

Don't Be Afraid of Your Own Power and of Using Power

Power is one of the most misunderstood ideas. Many of us have had the experience of power, both personally and through the observations of others and dramatization through the media, and have been led to believe that power is a bad word. The *misuse* of power—the use of power over someone or something else—deserves a bad rap. The power that I refer to here is the power that is inside of you: your ability to use your energy to influence outcomes. Find your power and use it wisely. When you find your power, it's ... powerful. Honor your own gift. Don't run away from it just because it's outside your comfort zone. Enduring power—power from the inside out—sustains and maintains. After you have found and honored your power, you then have to find the fine line between power and humility. The question

125

is—can you be both powerful and humble? The answer is—you have to be. The alternative—being powerful with no humility—easily slides into arrogance.

Don't Be Afraid to Share the Credit; Get a Partner

Don't buy into the ideas behind the old expression, "Lead, follow, or get out of the way." There are always many more options than those three, and decisions are not black or white, do or die. You'll learn a lot when working as a team. Or as Grover from *Sesame Street* said, "We'll have fun and get things done when we cooperate." The bottom line is that the sum of the parts *is* greater than the whole when there is teamwork. Successful players on a team are eager to ask questions and will get help from others around them in order to improve the team. Team players seek to motivate and inspire, and they put the needs of the group before their individual well-being. Your ability to ask for help, and other people's willingness to help you will affect your success more than you can alone.

Be part of a new paradigm of cooperation. Winning is something that you can do with a team. With a team, each member has a piece of the puzzle that can fit perfectly into what is needed. And the team doesn't have to be big. To make the most of your talents and time, recognize that you can't know everything, and take on a partner or build a team that's strong in the areas that you don't know. With a bit of synergy, you'll be able to create and accomplish more, and you'll find that the rocks in their heads fit the holes in yours.

Don't Just Succeed; Succeed by Helping Others Succeed

Success is not a one-person venture. Real success is inclusive of other people and also means helping other people succeed. Be sure to let other people shine. Successful leaders know how and when to delegate, as well. Successful delegation is about surrounding yourself with great people, knowing what their special skills are, and making best use of those skills.

It's quite a list. Certainly it's one I wish I'd had (and paid attention to) much earlier in life. As one example, time management somehow seemed unimportant and without consequences or penalties before my working life. So I have another recommendation to add to the list: Don't wait for any further explanation of these don'ts. Instead, make a point of practicing these ideas now, before more time passes. That's what it takes, as I learned early, and on the job at Men's Wearhouse.

Learning on the Run

Self-management was critical in the early days of Men's Wearhouse. There was always more to do than time to do it, so discipline in establishing priorities became key. By about 1976, the company had three, and then four stores; it was still in its infancy and growing. We had no "grand plan" other than opening more stores in Houston. We also didn't have the benefit of any of the fine management books that were written subsequently. We used what we thought was common sense and fairness in managing the company.

Back then, we did a little bit of everything. One moment we might have been discussing marketing and the next moment unpacking boxes and ticketing merchandise. If the manager of the store was out for lunch, one of us would come out of the office and work on the sales floor. While there were still only four stores, most days were similar. George and I would meet at the office in the back of store number one, make phone calls, sort through mail, and then head out to the other stores. We'd load up the car (or van, depending on which had more gas) with new merchandise and inter-store transfers, jump in, and go. We'd stop at each store, drop off the merchandise, and pick up paperwork. And we'd walk around: we'd talk to the employees, we'd talk to the customers, we'd look at the store, and we'd look through the merchandise.

This was guerilla research at its best, and a classic example of "Management by Walking Around" (MBWA)—the clever management technique described by Tom Peters and Robert Waterman, authors of *In Search of Excellence: Lessons from America's Best Run Companies*, in the 1980s. Cell phones were not ubiquitous, so while driving between stores, the two of us would talk about business—literally setting up the foundation for what was to come years later. We didn't put in sixteen-hour days, but we worked most every day, and even when we were not physically in the office, we were hanging out somewhere talking about the company. While we might have thought we were simply managing a small chain of men's clothing stores, what we were really doing was beginning to build something much larger and greater than either one us could probably have imagined at the time. It was, and is, an important lesson in management: we were managing each other, managing our company, managing our time, managing our expectations, and trying to manage the part of our lives that wasn't Men's Wearhouse. We had control over most, if not all, of it.

Managing Inside and Out

The lessons that I learned about self-management in those early days were important for me throughout my career at Men's Wearhouse, first on the floor as a worker and then, as the company and my responsibilities grew, as a manager and leader.

Know that one day, somehow, some way, you are going to be a leader—you will be called upon to lead *something*. You are going to be responsible for managing other people, whether at work, in a nonwork organization, or at home. Every day is an apprenticeship for that day that you become a leader. How are you going to lead? Start now. Learn now so that you will be prepared when the time comes. In the meantime, you *can* distinguish yourself so that you will be called upon to lead or manage. But before you lead, you're going to be *asked* to lead. How do you distinguish yourself so that you will be called upon?

Act like a leader by taking the initiative on new projects. Act like a leader by developing positive relationships with as many of your co-workers as you can. Act like a leader by working hard and not taking the easy way out. And finally, act like a leader by *acting like a leader*: by being the kind of person *you* would like to see in a leader.

Browse through the business section of any bookstore, and you'll find no shortage of books on leadership. Helpful as they are, these books are not going to teach you exactly how to lead. Leadership is not "one size fits all," and it's certainly not "one size fits all circumstances." But leadership does have a particular style. For some, it's an art; for others, it's war. Clearly, it's a challenge. And how you meet that challenge is the first step in what kind of leader you will ultimately become.

I prefer to think of leadership as an art, a war, and a style—all at the same time. Leadership is *in the moment*. There is no "right" style of leadership, because there is no "right" leader or person—employee or employer. There is *always* the right moment—it's *now*. The particular style is in the hands of the particular leader. What leadership really demands is presence, listening, and flexibility. I'll cover some personal leadership experiences and lessons and trust that they will be helpful in developing your *own* leadership style.

How Do You Become a Great Leader?

The Chinese Zen states that there are three essentials of leadership: humanity, clarity, and courage. I learned of these essentials through a book by Thomas Cleary called *Zen Lessons: The Art of Leadership* (at page 8). Yes, you'll find it grouped with today's leadership books. And its reliance on Zen serves as a reminder that leadership and leadership questions long predate the many current books on the market. Of the three essentials, clarity and courage can be taught, although not easily. It's the humanity part that has to be developed—with effort and over time, a long time.

To be a great leader, think of the most basic and cherished human values, values that start early in life. What do children crave? Love, attention, and recognition. Few of us get enough, and we bring into adulthood a sense of loss and sadness from this reality. For some people, this sense is overt; for others, it's covert. In either case, the sadness can be a drain and a strain on people's ability to grow. As adults, these childhood needs might be rephrased: people want to feel that they are respected, visible, and acknowledged, that they are held and heard. These needs come right back to love, attention, and recognition—all of which can be found and shared, especially if you're going to lead.

How can you do this? Again, there is no one size fits all. But understand that to become a great leader, you will need to be flexible, surround yourself with great people, learn from others, let others shine, delegate responsibility, nourish creativity, and reach out to the disaffected.

BE FLEXIBLE

Being a great leader means that you have to be a child, a student, a warrior, a teacher, and a parent—all at once. It's about being present enough to know what hat you're going to have to put on, depending on the circumstance.

- Be a child. You have to have a child's innate curiosity, the willingness to experiment, to not let the "past" be your guide. And you have to be willing to take risks.
- Be a student. Be open, be interested, and be always willing to listen. If you are, you'll see that there are lessons all around—especially from your co-workers.

- Be a warrior. Sometimes you have to go it alone—fighting for your idea, for your company, or for yourself.
- Be a teacher. You have to teach every day. This teaching can be literal: by explaining what you're doing. This teaching can be by example: letting others see how you manage and how you lead.
- Be a parent. The people who report to you often end up looking to you for more than leadership. At times you represent the authority that they might have missed in their lives. Keep their needs for love, attention, and recognition in mind and help to fulfill those needs in ways appropriate to the business setting.

In all of these, you need to mentally adapt to each situation as a new experience and remain flexible when reasoning and problem solving.

SURROUND YOURSELF WITH GREAT PEOPLE

Everyone has their own special skill. Think of that as good news and know that you aren't going to be—and needn't be—the best at every aspect of the organization. Find the best people that you can at every level of the organization, and reward them. Don't allow yourself to be threatened by someone, but rather be heartened by their existence. Leadership is about only one ability—being a leader. It's not about being the best, the smartest, the most clever, or getting things done single-handedly. By finding the best and the brightest, you can develop synergy at all levels. People look to the leader for how to lead themselves. When they witness synergistic leadership, they pass on synergistic leadership, thus strengthening the entire organization.

LEARN FROM OTHERS

You've got great people around you. Learn from them. Successful leaders learn from everyone, and they put personal power second to the overall well-being of the company. They know that management is not control—it's collaboration. Great leaders focus on the team instead of being inaccessible figures perched high on a pedestal. Leaders learn along the way and know they can never stop learning. Their information can come from many sources: formal education, business experiences, employees—and keeping their eyes and ears open all of the time.

Every once in a while, even if you don't need to, ask someone else, "What do *you* think?" Sure, you might have already made up your mind or have a strong feeling about the subject, but if you remember that there's always more information in front of you than in you, there's a chance that you'll hear something new. Besides, it's an opportunity to solicit another person to engage in conversation.

Learn to embrace feedback wholeheartedly. Be open to the idea that someone else has an idea that might be better than yours. Learn to learn.

LET OTHER PEOPLE SHINE

Lao Tzu, the Chinese Taoist philosopher, once remarked, "Of the best leaders, when their task is accomplished, the people all remark,

'We have done it ourselves.'" When I first read that many years ago, I wrote it down and taped it to my phone at the office, so that I'd never forget it. It is what leadership is all about: letting other people shine. It's about training people to one day come in and take over *your* job, so that you can move on to bigger things. If you're already a leader, how much more do you need to shine? Is your need to shine more valuable than the importance of reaching out and helping someone else? If it is, then whoever you are and however you became a leader, you need to step back and reevaluate.

I learned at least part of this lesson back in my junior year of high school when I was president of the Hazleton Temple youth group. It was a small group, and we were good—so good that we were voted the best youth group in our region (Northeastern Pennsylvania). This feather in my cap was supposed to lead me onto bigger and better things—like being the president of the Northeastern Region of Temple youth groups in my senior year. However, I wasn't nominated. I was shocked. I had been *sure* that I would be. I had a proven track record of leadership and success, and so as far as I was concerned, all of the parts added up. When I found out who *was* nominated, I was furious—until I spent a bit of time thinking about the whole situation, especially the person who was nominated.

He was a friend of mine, someone I had met a year earlier and shared not only good times but also good conversation with. He was bright, energetic, and had many qualities that I greatly admired. Even though other people encouraged me to run against him, I decided against it. Why? Because I thought he'd do a better job than I would have, and I told him so. Not only did he run, and I didn't, but I supported him in the election, and he won. It was a defining moment in both of our lives. And although we now live on opposite coasts, we remain friends and in contact with each other more than forty years later.

Long after this experience, I learned that sharing love, attention, and recognition is part of "team building" and part of creating the "family" at work. One of the most important (and, quite frankly, fun) aspects to team building and leadership is learning how to create that space that lets other people shine. It's that space that lets others wake up, realize, and appreciate their own special gifts and their own contributions. Let the people who report to you reach for their own stars. And be sure that they get the credit when they do. Don't worry about yourself. In the end, if all things are fair and even, their successes will reflect well on you.

If you can do good deeds for others from a genuine place of kindness and without expectations, it inspires others to do the same and makes the work environment a kinder place. Your selfless giving and credit to others are seeds that your teammates will return to you as blossoms. Make an effort to regularly thank and praise your co-workers, for the little things and the big things. The same applies for your partner and your children. The sentiments take only seconds to express, but will be long remembered and appreciated—when they're genuine.

In addition to letting other people shine, you also have to let them slip. They have to find their own space, make their own mistakes, and then learn from those mistakes. Sometimes when you do this, you create a situation where a decision is not the best decision in the short term for the company. Then what? My experience is that generally,

135

if it doesn't appear as if it's going to hurt the company in the long run, it's okay, because what's equally important is the growth of the individual. As a manager and a leader, this is a decision you have to make—most often, in the moment.

DELEGATE RESPONSIBILITY

You *may* be able to do everything, but you don't *have* to. If you trust other people to help you out, you'll contribute to the overall morale and growth of the team. Even though you might not be sure that a specific person you're delegating to can handle the task, delegate it anyway. Doing so can be a great experience in stretching someone else's capabilities, and the task can be a great learning experience as well.

NURTURE CREATIVITY

In his delightful and informative book, called *Orbiting the Giant Hairball,* Gordon MacKenzie argues that, like a cat accumulates a hairball, an organization accumulates all its collective thoughts, rules, and regulations. This ungainly hairball becomes part of the corporate structure. Unfortunately, over time, any organization can get completely caught up in itself, like a hairball. MacKenzie worked at Hallmark cards for thirty years, so he can speak from experience about the hairball. However, he wasn't the CEO—he was a great follower and evidently a great manager.

The idea of orbiting means that at all times, you have to pay attention and make sure that you're not getting all caught up in the company "hairball" at the expense of your own creativity and the creativity of others. Orbiting means extricating yourself from the hairball and allowing yourself to follow your dreams and even your whims. A whim comes from the most creative part of your being that has an enormous amount of energy and force. You can always reject a whim later, but it's easier to change lanes once you're moving than from a dead stop.

REACH OUT TO THE DISAFFECTED

Learn how to love your enemies. Why? No one else is going to tell you the truth. It doesn't get much simpler than that. You are going to learn more, if you really listen, from the people who oppose you than from the people who support you. The key is listening. ***Stop!*** Think about it. Think of the people on your team. It probably seems to them as though it's in their best interest, and perhaps yours, to support you and your ideas. Where the window opens—if you let it—is when you can learn from the people who are opposed to your idea. True, sometimes others are opposed to your ideas because they are opposed to you in general, but most of the time, people are opposed to your ideas because they have ideas of their own. Those ideas are valid—just as valid as yours.

> *Learn from the people who are opposed to your idea.*

The disaffected—those people who continue to oppose you, especially those who do so vocally—are the ones with the potential create havoc. You have to learn to reach out to them. Doing so is the ultimate test of your management skills. The vast majority of these people are bright and decent, but somewhere along the line, they got lost in frustration, anger, or confusion. It's not an easy task, but if you can focus on finding the good in these people, you have a chance at educating and inspiring them. When you're successful at this, you will have really helped to create something great. You'll know it at the time and perhaps soon find that those "disaffected" are now the most energetic and eager members of your team. This is something I found out, in a big way, back in college, as the next story explains.

Lesson Learned: Turning Confrontation into Cooperation

In my junior year at Rutgers, I was president of my fraternity, Zeta Beta Tau (ZBT). I did it for three reasons. Ever looking for a way to make a buck, and ever conscious of the fact that I didn't want to saddle all of my college expenses on my parents, I knew that being president meant free room, board, and fraternity dues. But more than that, I had so enjoyed my sophomore year living in the house that I wanted to spread the word, not only to attract new brothers to ZBT, but also to polish up the reputation for all fraternities on campus. Perhaps, though, the most compelling reason I became president was that no one else wanted to. It was a thankless job that had only one reward: the free ride.

In the process of going over the finances shortly after I became president, I discovered a massive scam involving money, food, and kickbacks in the kitchen, which was the single largest source of income and expense for the fraternity. I was faced with not only confronting the suspected brothers, but also having to raise dues and board to cover the missing funds. I called an emergency meeting of the house to try to articulate the dire situation. But concern quickly turned to chaos, and I became the focus of several of my fraternity brothers' wrath. They were not at all pleased with the increased fees. At one especially heated point in the meeting, a fellow brother stood up and haughtily asked, "Is this a fraternity or is it a business?" I looked him straight in the eye and said, "For *you*, it's whatever you want. But you have elected me as your president and for *me*, it's a fraternity *and* a business." Dues had to be raised, and I had to deal with the fraternity brothers who had taken the money *and* with the many disenchanted fraternity brothers, who were seriously considering quitting.

As I began to feel the "brotherhood" unraveling, I decided to take a gamble and try to entice some particularly disaffected brothers into the fold. I had read about the success another ZBT chapter had with an ingenious idea for fund-raising—a dance marathon. I approached my fraternity brothers and convinced them that this was something that ZBT could do to become a better part of the overall Rutgers community. I convinced them that it was something much more than a weekend party, or any of the other aspects of fraternity life that some of these brothers so abhorred. I suggested that they work as a team, put together a plan, and see what developed. Although hesitant at first, the more the group talked and worked on the project, the more they liked it. The more they liked it, the harder they worked at it. The harder they worked, the easier it all came together.

The rules for the marathon were pretty simple: organizations on campus would sponsor a couple and raise money for that couple.

The winning couple was the one whose backing organization raised the most money. Both the winning organization and the winning couple would receive prizes, but the money they raised would go to the American Cancer Society. The marathon itself was made very easy for the couples to live through. The point wasn't to get them to fall over; the point was to have their organizations go out and raise the money on their behalf.

Everything for the event—the prizes for the couples, advertising, food, and entertainment—had to be donated. The members of ZBT solicited it all. We convinced Rutgers to loan us the gym for the weekend at no charge, but they insisted on a security deposit of $5,000—no small sum in 1971. This deposit became a bit of a sticking point. The American Cancer Society couldn't put the deposit up; doing so was against *their* charter. ZBT couldn't put up the deposit; doing so was against *our* charter. But, as President, I looked the other way and wrote out a check, with the assurance from Rutgers that it would be cashed only if there was damage done to the gym—and that, in any case, it wouldn't be cashed before the weekend ended.

My most vivid recollection of the weekend was a moment about thirty minutes before the marathon began. We had just finished preparing the fifty or so couples as to what was going to occur and sent them off to another room to rest up. Like dutiful soldiers, the fraternity committee members were busy with last-minute details, leaving me alone in the empty gym. As I sat on the stage of the darkened room gazing at the reflection of the lights shining on a mirrored ball suspended from the ceiling, I sighed, smiled, and shook my head, knowing that this event was either going to be a roaring success or a colossal flop. I knew that I had done the best *I* could. I knew that my fraternity brothers had done the best that *they* could. All we could do was sit back and wait. It was a scary, yet tremendously enervating moment.

My fear of failure caused me to blank out on the next two hours. The next recollection I have of that evening was being in a room adjacent to the gym that was set up as the central site for collecting the money. A knock on the door brought with it a demand from campus patrol wanting to know who was in charge. All eyes and heads turned to me as I sheepishly answered, "I guess I am." "We have a problem," I was informed. Dozens of potential problems raced through my mind, but not this one—crowd control. There were *so many* people in the gym watching the event that campus patrol had to start turning them away at the door. In fact, there were so many people in the gym that we couldn't get out of the room to see them. The gym was a madhouse, and the street in front of the gym was an even greater madhouse.

One of the other "problems" that we hadn't anticipated was what to do with the money that was being raised. Much of it was cash, and much of the cash was change. Several hours later, and long past midnight, four of us, with Campus Patrol in tow, rolled a footlocker loaded with money (mostly change) down College Avenue in New Brunswick. We knew that the event had been a smashing success. I, for one, had a new appreciation for the word "brotherhood." We were all tired and spent, but we knew we had been part of something really great.

From this experience, I learned a few things about leadership, lessons that have stayed with me ever since:

- **Reaching out to the disaffected brings everyone closer.** The brothers who organized the marathon could just as easily have left the fraternity. They barely liked the idea of fraternity, and they were the most vocal about the dues increase. By including them in a new project, I was able to re-energize their spirits as individuals and get them to reach out to other brothers for help and cooperation.

- **Synergy.** The entire event was organized by a handful of people. They worked hard, and they worked well— together. They had a common goal, didn't let their egos get involved, and accomplished far more by working harmoniously than I could ever have hoped for. Their efforts became contagious, so much so that the weekend of the event, nearly every one of the one hundred-plus members of the fraternity were present and working. It was a proud moment for all of us.

- **You can make your point, but you don't have to MAKE YOUR POINT.** The brothers who stole the money knew that they had been caught red-handed. They offered up no excuses or explanations, nor did they offer to pay the money back. I decided that the best thing to do was to let them quietly remove themselves from the fraternity. While the fraternity had every right to press charges, I didn't think it was right to jeopardize their futures. They knew they had done something wrong, and, as far as I was concerned, that was enough.

One of the other important aspects to leadership is creating something that is lasting. By taking positive action in the face of a crisis, we established the dance marathon as a fundraiser, one that, more than thirty-five years later, is still an annual event at Rutgers.

Yet another part of leadership includes effective problem-solving and creating an environment that encourages it. The starting point for problem solving is the realization that all outer problems have inner solutions, as you'll see in the next chapter.

7

All Outer Problems Have Inner Solutions

MANY OF US ARE GUILTY of falling into the trap of assuming that the problems in our own lives emanate from the outside. It's a natural inclination, but that perception is backwards; instead, life—*your* life—is an inside job. Everything about your life begins from the inside—inside of you—including any outer problems. And the solution to all of your outer problems also rests inside of one place—you.

Everyone encounters problems in life, but it doesn't mean that life itself is a problem. Quite the contrary—life is an experience to be lived. The necessary bumps along the way, and your ability to counter, recover, and learn from them are all part of that experience. *Stop!* Think for a moment about your own problems. Isolate the biggest one of them at this moment and ask yourself the following questions:

- How did it become a problem?
- Who are the contributors to the problem?

- Do you continue to do things to contribute to the problem?
- Who is going to solve it?
- How is it going to be solved?

Obviously, these are questions for which only you have the answer, but at a more global and simplistic level, there is one answer—you. You are the source of any problems that you have, you maintain these problems, and you're the one who is going to have to solve them. This is a "learn it now or learn it later" lesson—and you'll do yourself a great service by learning it now. This chapter will help you redirect your effort to approach and solve problems from your inside, using many of the tools articulated earlier in this book.

But first, a little side trip. In chapter 4, I talked about meditation and hinted at what was to come as relates to yoga. Well, here it comes. Once again, invoke the five-minute rule. That should give you enough time to read about what has become an important part of my life, and a way to solve mental as well as physical problems. Who knows? It might become an important part of your life as well.

An Inner Journey

We all have personal horror stories—things that have happened in our lives that, upon looking back years later, we said, "How did I get through that?" One of mine follows. As for the situation that caused the horror story, in retrospect I can now also say, "What was I thinking?"

January 4, 1998. There aren't a lot of times in my life in which I've asked the universe for a specific favor—one just for me. On this day,

I did. I asked for help to not to feel what I was feeling so that I could safely drive from San Diego, the place I had called home for two short years, to San Francisco, the place that had been my occasional home for the same two years. I needed help to literally keep me on the road for the long drive that marked the end of a relationship. It didn't matter that many years later I would realize the relationship had been ill-fated and misguided. In that moment, it felt like my dreams and hopes were over. I was left with failure and fear—failure based on the past, and fear of the future. The present was a long drive ahead of me to San Francisco, to begin to pick up the pieces of my life.

January 14, 1998. There is a belief in yoga that the teacher arrives when the student is ready. On this day, I was ready. Just ten days after returning to San Francisco, my misery and I headed over to the club where I worked out. I had tried to make it a habit to exercise late in the day, in an effort to exhaust myself enough so that I could sleep and again to not feel. On this night, after finishing my workout, and on the way out of the gym, I peered into the yoga studio and noticed several men and women on their mats, preparing for a class. "Why not?" the little voice in my head urged, and fortunately, I ignored the opposing voices.

And on this night, my teacher presented herself to me. Since then, I've practiced yoga and meditation with Kristen—learning a new way to breathe, learning a new way to feel, and learning a new way to approach the world. The pain that I felt on the night that I met Kristen didn't miraculously disappear, but my way of *dealing* with the pain began to. I had found an inspirational teacher who helped open the inner solution to what at the time felt like a monumental outer problem.

I can't promise any such wonder for you if you begin a yoga practice, but I can promise you this: *something* will happen. I don't profess to be a master or a guru—I am merely a student, who continues to practice. I'm one of the many people whose lives have changed because of the practice of yoga. As I began to integrate the practice of yoga with who and what I was, I began to find more peace and equanimity in my life. Yoga has also made me a better partner, a better parent, and a better businessman.

Yoga literally means union—union with yourself. Yoga is a five-thousand-year-old technique for spiritual development. It isn't a religion or a stylish exercise regimen; it's a way of living, by integrating three key elements—posture, breathing, and mindfulness. Yoga can help you find that place between your external physical self (your body) and your inner self (your emotions, your mindset, and even your soul) where you can develop discipline and find peace, serenity, and happiness. Yoga is one of the ways of unlocking the answers that you already have.

You don't need to be in shape to begin a practice of yoga—in fact, the most important thing you need is an open mind. Interestingly enough, through a practice of yoga, you will be able to develop a *more* open mind.

> *Through a practice of yoga, you will be able to develop a more open mind.*

To my mind, there are six basic aspects of yoga that make it a very attractive practice and spill over nicely to how you might consider *handling* your life; these are:

1. There's no competition, either with others or with yourself.
   The best you can do on any one day is simply that—the

best that you can do. It has nothing to do with what you might have done on another day and nothing to do with what anyone else in a class might be doing. You learn by listening, watching yourself, and being patient and kind with yourself.

2. Yoga forces you to stay within yourself, and it teaches you boundaries about yourself. It teaches you to find your greatness, one day at a time.

3. There is no judgment in yoga; you learn how to just "be."

4. The practice of yoga helps you to develop self-reliance, to harness all parts of your being, and to give you the capacity to take care of yourself, especially in times of crisis.

5. Yoga is about achieving subtle results, both physically and mentally. If you lift weights or do any muscle-building work, you can see the results in the literal increase and tone of your muscles. In yoga, the results are less obvious, but over time, you'll acquire a more toned body. Beyond the physical, there are the mental benefits. Find out for yourself—just once, go to a yoga class. You'll walk out of your first class feeling calm, rested, and with a much different perspective on the world than you had going in.

6. Yoga is called a practice. You will never see an Olympic yoga event, you'll never get a trophy for "Most Improved Yogi." All you will ever do is practice. It's all about being present. It's a great lesson that's fantastic to implement with the rest of your life.

Since yoga is a discipline of the body and the mind, its benefits naturally translate into your relationships—both personal and professional. Because, after all, what your life is about is discovery and re-discovery, and if these tools can help take you to the place that once was safe, then it's worth the trip.

In a certain way, yoga is a wonderful metaphor for a lot of what I've been trying to speak to in this book: not only are the answers inside of you, but they're also connected to a part of you that you may have abandoned long ago—your childhood. It is in childhood that you were most free, light, and perfectly flexible (mentally and physically). It is in childhood that you may have been fearless (or nearly), because you then had no frame of reference from which fear or inflexibility could manifest. Yoga, if not this book, can help you to rediscover that freedom and the light that you had as a child.

A Journey through Life

In your inner journey and your journey in life, you will encounter problems and find solutions. In order to be more proficient at working out those solutions, you need to first understand the nature of problems.

ENCOUNTERING PROBLEMS

Among the many choices you have in your life, when it comes to problems, the choice comes down to this: How are you going to live? Are you going to live with problems and drama, or are you going to live in peace? Here's a little help with that conundrum—choose peace. Start from a place of peace within yourself and try to create peaceful coexistences. You've already been given the tools and two great practices—meditation and yoga. When you start from a place of peace, you set the stage for problem *solving* rather than problem creating. Not only that, but you also create an environment around you that is less problem-filled to begin with—one where you *attract* fewer problems.

Problems encourage us to invent solutions and draw out of us inspired thoughts and insights, but only if we are present and willing to open our minds to creative thought. Part of the nature of problems is to show us the parts of ourselves that are yet to be mastered. We all mature and grow at different speeds and what might be a problem for one person is something easily solved by another. Think of a problem as a "pop quiz"—it's going to generally come when you least expect it and when you are least prepared. Despite how it may feel at the time, problems do have a purpose. You're not better off if you avoid them; you are better off if you don't look for blame and if you don't label others.

Problems Have Purpose. There is a purpose to problems: they are a blessing on many levels. They are there for your benefit, to help you create, to bring out your creative genius, and to help you to grow. They exist as a way for you to constantly check in with yourself; to make sure that you are grounded, present, aware, and in touch with all that is around you. They require you to use your imagination and tap into a sense of yourself that you might not often rely on. You are always in a state of "becoming"; there is no endpoint. Can you be comfortable with being uncomfortable? You have no choice; like the rest of the plant and animal world, you're either growing or you're dying. Choose to grow. Problems are part of that growth.

Avoidance Won't Work. When you avoid problems, you are setting yourself up for receiving them back again one day, this time with penalties and interest. All too often, when ignored, problems tend to magnify and get exponentially worse. *Stop!* Think about some old problem that you ignored. Did it get better on its own or worse? Probably, it got worse. When a problem arises, attack it—with every bit of your being. You'll find a great lesson, if you pay attention.

This Is a Test. You are always going to be tested in life, even long after you're out of school. The tests may come from the least expected places; they also come from the places where you need the most amount of work, those places that are least developed in your consciousness. Have you noticed that the same problems keep arising in your life, only from different sources? Maybe it's relationships—you've been in and out of several but just can't seem to get it "right." That's the universe's way of testing you and bringing you back to square one—and you'll be tested until you get it right. Everything that you do, every thought that you have, and every outward expression that you make counts as a building block, preparing you for the tests. Hold onto your truth, hold onto your integrity, and hold onto your heart, and you will be guided in the right direction. Pay attention. Be present.

Here's a way to deal with a problem and begin to solve it while being "in the moment." I call it, "The mantra of the air raid alert." Radio and television stations occasionally run signals as tests in case of an emergency. At the conclusion of the test, the announcer declares, "This has been a test of the emergency broadcast system. In the event of a real emergency ..." Think of any problem as a test—only a test—of your own emergency broadcast system, of your ability to come up with a creative solution. Dealing with problems as they come up—not avoiding them—is your assurance of keeping the "real emergency" at bay.

Blaming Doesn't Help. What is the first thing you do when you spot a problem or when you see something gone wrong? If you're like most of us, your first move is to think, "Whose fault is it?" This question is usually followed by blame. And the blame is not usually directed toward yourself. Blame has a misdirected and tragic underpinning—it assumes that you sit in a position to dole out judgment. This self-appointed position gives you the power (as in negative power) to be ultimate arbiter of the behavior of other people. It's a terrible throne to sit on, because there is nowhere to go from there. Attributing blame is a no-win situation that leaves everyone involved depleted and reactive. Rather than start from a place of *blame*, start from a place of *solution*. Blame may get you temporary freedom, but eventually, you're going to have to confront the problem, deal with it in a reasonable manner, come up with a solution, and then move on. Skipping blame allows you to get to the solution faster and to learn the lesson in a peaceful way.

Don't Label Others. Chances are you label others without realizing it. Just as often as we needlessly label ourselves, we also place unnecessary labels on the people around us. How many times have you ignored someone because you've already labeled him as a "nuisance" (or worse)? Here's a novel thought: we're *all* a "nuisance"—sometimes. Think about this: "sometimes" is the same as "existential"—how we are in any one moment. "Always" is how we essentially are. Few people are nuisances all of the time. When you automatically apply "always" to people, you avoid getting to really know them, and instead, you make judgments about them from a distance. Learn how to *really* see people so we can better get along and work in harmony with them. Pay attention to the person you consider a nuisance. Wonder about the possibility that he might be your polar opposite and that there may be great synergy in that. Remember that the rest of the world and that nuisance are pretty much like you: we all want to be loved, desire freedom, want happiness, want to be visible, and desire peace. Be a generator of all of these, and your actions will come back to you with interest. Be a labeler and that will also come back to you—with penalties that can cost you.

People label others in interpersonal dealings, at work with co-workers, and at work with customers. In the retail business, labeling a customer is about the biggest error that can be committed on the sales floor. Every person who walks in the door of any store is a potential lifetime customer.

I once had the opportunity to explain this to the senior management of Bergdorf Goodman, a division of Neiman Marcus. The then-president of Bergdorf's men's store had asked that I speak about customer service to the group. In retrospect, he deserves a lot of credit for asking me to speak. It was an admission on his part that the esteemed store he was running didn't have one very important aspect well done. The president didn't know me personally, but he knew the reputation of Men's Wearhouse. I felt that my speaking didn't exactly amount to divulging any top-secret information, especially since Men's Wearhouse had no stores in the New York area at the time and our customer base was rather different. For my part, I was honored that Men's Wearhouse was so well thought of.

Two days before I spoke, I decided to go to the store and experience it as a customer. I went there with a seven-year-old boy who was the son of a friend of mine and who *really* had to go to the bathroom. The sales force in the store avoided me like the plague and were only too happy to usher us to the bathroom and then out the front door. The next day I walked into the store by myself, wearing a suit—a Men's Wearhouse suit, naturally. Strangely enough, I was treated the same way. The sales force apparently didn't think I looked like I had what it took to be a Bergdorf customer. And I doubt that it was just about the suit; it could have been that I just didn't appear to be hip enough.

The day after that was the day that I spoke to the senior management. Again, I wore a Men's Wearhouse suit and before I started my presentation, I asked the group a question: "If I came into your store today looking like I do, would you wait on me?" The answers around the room were, "Of course, yes!" My next questions were: "Why didn't you yesterday? Why didn't you the day before?" These were rhetorical questions, but I think I had made my point. It was then very easy for me to convey a basic rule in retail and in life: don't judge a book by its cover. A retail business is not the place to be judging people. It is about treating them all the same way—with respect, regardless of what you might think about their appearance or demeanor. In business, as in life, what you see on the surface is not necessarily what is really there.

The best that could be said about Bergdorf's service at that time was that it was consistent—consistently bad. As I looked out at the people in the room that day, I noticed that they all appeared to be wearing clothing from Bergdorf—and they all looked much hipper than I did. But once I had their attention I broached the thought that the hip factor might have been at the root of their judgment. My talk seemed to go well, but I had little feedback. I left the meeting wondering what they were going to do and knowing that only time would tell.

Several months later, I walked into the store as a "customer," and this time I was treated very well. Ditto for the next few trips to the store. Honestly, I don't know what Bergdorf did specifically to improve their service, but I know that they listened. Whatever they did, they did it very well and very consistently. I can only hope that my hour or so talk made a difference. Either way, I was just a catalyst. Someone got the message and made sure that the quality of help at Bergdorf Goodman was the same as the quality of their merchandise. With the problem in sight, someone (more likely many someones) solved it. Similarly, now that you have a sense of the nature and challenge of problems, you're ready to tackle solutions.

UNCOVERING SOLUTIONS

Embedded in every problem is the solution, and generally, it's a solution that you already know. What do you need to find the solution? Patience, your own knowledge, and sometimes a little help from the outside. And more. Before you can even begin to solve a problem, you have to recognize that there is one to begin with. This is easier said than done, especially if it's a personal problem (such as addiction). Recognizing that there even *is* a problem often requires you to be open, honest, and present with yourself.

Shed the Past. Once you've established that there is a problem, don't dwell on it. Instead, use that energy to begin to create a solution. If you're in a group situation, don't let the "collective wisdom of negatives" take over. This dangerous group dynamic dwells on the problem and not the solution, often making matters far worse.

When thinking about a solution, a great way to begin is to eliminate two words: *always* and *never*. What does *always* get you? "Why, we *always* do it this way. Every time we do *this*… we *always* get *that* as a result." Always is the lazy way out, the path of least resistance, the universal cure-all for unimaginative thinking, and the absolute guarantee of mediocrity. Allow yourself to thrive on change and invention, and it will make for a more organic way to solve a problem. And quite frankly, it'll be more *fun*. If there has to be an always, let it be always challenging the status quo—yours and others.

> *Allow yourself to thrive on change and invention.*

What does the word *never* get you? "We *never* do …" Never is the guarantee that all conversation will come to a standstill. Like the word *always*, *never* traps you in the box of no creative thought or expression. Worse, since with the word *never* comes the implied threat of reprisal if you actually *do* break a rule.

If you want to create new paradigms for your life, one of the best ways to do so is to break free of the past. The only way to change the future is to not bring the past into the present. The very concepts of always and never are rooted in the past. Learn to invent present solutions to create a better future.

Calm, Quiet Confidence for the Future. Sometimes the solution to a problem arrives with quiet and inner confidence. Every now and then you don't have to bowl people over with your knowledge or your thoughts; sometimes just being yourself is more than enough. While I didn't fully realize it at the time, I saw the value in this a very long time ago.

When I arrived at Rutgers for my first day, I realized one thing that would have been obvious, had I thought it out beforehand: I knew absolutely no one on campus. Most of the other guys in my dorm section knew several other people on campus. In fact, many of them had gone to high school together and had chosen each other as roommates. I knew no one—not a soul in my dorm or in the entire university system. I knew no one in the state of New Jersey, for that matter. I felt lost, adrift, and downright scared. It was a problem that only I was going to solve, and I had no choice but to move on. Shaken though I was, I realized that I could solve another problem simultaneously by reinventing myself. It was a chance to leave all of the labels I had grown up with back in Hazleton and start with a clean slate in New Brunswick. Even so, settling into my dorm room and meeting my roommate and everyone else in the dorm was overwhelming. As a classic small-town boy thrown into the big school environment, I was dazed but determined to gut my way through it.

The first night, everyone in the dorm gathered for a meeting, outlining the do's and don'ts of dorm living. Later, each floor of the dorm got together for a smaller meeting. We went around the room and introduced ourselves, delivering a statement of who we were and what brought us to Rutgers. We then had to elect a floor representative, someone who would serve on the board of the dorm, organizing events, creating policy, etc. There I sat, knowing no more than the name of anyone other than my roommate. Next thing I know, *I* was elected the floor representative. Four months later, I was elected president of my fraternity pledge class under very similar circumstances. Once again, when it came time to select a leader, the thirty or so guys all turned to me. In both cases, I asked myself, "Why me?" The answer didn't come until many years later when I realized it had been more than naïveté that was emanating from me; it was honesty and quiet leadership. By then I'd learned that leading with quietness and solving problems by just being me was all that I needed.

Stay Calm; Work in Harmony. When you're calm, you are most receptive to new thoughts and ideas. It's a great start to solving problems while working with others. Solving problems requires your internal harmony, and it requires you to be in harmony with the people you are working with on the solution. You don't have to be in the problem by yourself. And you shouldn't assume you know where others are in their lives or their problems. Instead, ask questions, and understand where people are coming from before you begin to go about problem-solving with them. If you don't get caught up in the

159

problem, if you seek out help and guidance from others, often you'll see that the solution is a lot easier to find.

Give It Time. Today's huge problem might be something you end up laughing at tomorrow. Or, as my grandfather, Sam Goldman, used to say: "Today is the tomorrow you were worried about yesterday." Sometimes the best solution to a problem is to let it marinate for a bit—to look at it later on when you might have a fresher perspective—to make sure that you're acting, not reacting to the situation.

Moving Past the Solution

When a problem is solved and the crisis is over, there are two more processes to go through to ensure that you learn the most you can from the problem and move forward.

Practice Failing, Forgiving, and Forgetting: 3 Fs. You might have made a mistake that caused the problem. Deal with it, be strong enough to admit your mistake, and move on. We all make mistakes—some are more magnificent than others.

If the mistake was yours, forgive yourself—you're only human. If others were clearly part of it, forgive them as well. They too are only human. If you really want personal freedom, then forgiveness is the path to it. We are all perfectly imperfect. Forgiveness releases you from the demons of guilt, shame, and remorse. If you don't forgive, these demons will eat away at you. They will steal the sacred commodities that you have: time, peace, and freedom.

Being freed from the past gives you the ability to forget. Being freed from the past gives you the power to be in the now—to be present. Don't hold a grudge—either against yourself or someone else. Despite your best efforts, you will make many more mistakes and if you let yourself get too tied up in any one mistake, you won't recover well enough to tackle the next problem.

Learn the Lesson. Take a step back and appreciate what you've done in solving the problem and realize the lessons you've learned, so that you don't repeat the problem. Certainly we had plenty of opportunities for lessons at Men's Wearhouse, as the next section highlights.

Lesson Learned:
Stay Calm and Stick to Your Knitting

When I was the general merchandise manager at Men's Wearhouse, I tried to stay focused—and to keep employees focused—on what customers wanted and expected to find in the stores. Questions over the merchandise selection constantly underscored the importance of patience—especially mine. Well-meaning employees would often suggest that we sell everything from life insurance to surf gear. My answer was most often "No," and I had to politely explain that while we *could* sell anything in the stores, the real question was always *should* we be selling it. Then I proceeded to talk about snow tires, explaining that I believed that if we had snow tires in our stores, we'd sell them— but not enough of them to pay the rent and other expenses, and that snow tires weren't what the company did *best,* and that selling them wouldn't be enhancing the Men's Wearhouse brand.

The company was clearly successful at capturing the wallet of Baby Boomer men when it came to dress apparel. Many years ago, we thought: we're good at men's clothes; why not women's? Since we already had women shopping in our stores, either with or for a man in their lives, we thought it would be a natural. We very quickly discovered that selling women's clothing was *much* easier said than done. It was a disaster. We lacked the merchandising talent and had no understanding of how women shopped for clothing. We did nothing right other than have the good sense to stop and cut our losses.

A more recent foray into something new, however, turned out differently and was a great example of "sticking to our knitting." One of the things that I used to lose sleep over was how the company was going to attract the *next* generation entering the workplace. Several years ago, the man who was then the District Manager in Seattle came up with the idea of renting tuxedos in Men's Wearhouse stores. He had done some research and thought the idea made sense—or at least enough sense to warrant giving it a try. "Go ahead, give it a whirl," we told him. We created a small infrastructure to make it happen, and we began renting tuxedos in the Seattle stores.

At first, the employees in the stores resisted because we were also *selling* tuxedos. Furthermore, renting tuxedos was a paperwork headache for the sales force and a merchandising challenge for the company. It was one thing to sell inventory that was housed in a store; it was quite a different thing to rent inventory that was stored in a warehouse hundreds, if not thousands, of miles away. Both were examples of potential impediments to success—they weren't reasons for not trying to make an apparently good idea succeed. For a few years, the company stumbled as it got used to a whole new way of doing business. Soon enough, something magical happened: the concept began to work, the impediments decreased, in large part thanks to technology, and—as we had expected—the rental customer who came into the stores was a *different* person than the customer who bought a tuxedo and a person who otherwise might never have stepped into a Men's Wearhouse store. The rental program turned out to be a giant success, and Men's Wearhouse capitalized on what it was already proficient in—customer service, advertising, sourcing of merchandise, and distribution. The stores got to benefit from the tuxedo rental, additional traffic in the form of high school students renting for proms, and younger men renting for weddings.

By 2007, tuxedo rentals had become a business with revenues in excess of $100 million for Men's Wearhouse. And in early 2007, the company completed a transaction of a chain of tuxedo rental stores, making Men's Wearhouse the largest renter of tuxedos in the country. This was a great example of taking an external problem (whether the company was going to outlive its customer base) and creating an internal solution (expanding the brand through a logical merchandise extension). It was also a great example of overcoming resistance through tenacity and hard work and an example of patience overcoming force. It was a case of successful experimentation in something new that was well worth the effort, risk, and expense.

The lesson? Sometimes it helps to "go with the flow" and to appreciate that you control your own destiny. It's a lot easier when you have a little wind in your sails. That wind can be in the form of practicing presence, listening, yoga, or meditation. These are also tools that will help you implement the rest of the ideas in this book.

concept began to work, the impediments decreased, in large part thanks to technology, and—as we had expected—the rental customer who came into the stores was a *different* person than the customer who bought a tuxedo and a person who otherwise might never have stepped into a Men's Wearhouse store. The rental program turned out to be a giant success, and Men's Wearhouse capitalized on what it was already proficient in—customer service, advertising, sourcing of merchandise, and distribution. The stores got to benefit from the tuxedo rental, additional traffic in the form of high school students renting for proms, and younger men renting for weddings.

By 2007, tuxedo rentals had become a business with revenues in excess of $100 million for Men's Wearhouse. And in early 2007, the company completed a transaction of a chain of tuxedo rental stores, making Men's Wearhouse the largest renter of tuxedos in the country. This was a great example of taking an external problem (whether the company was going to outlive its customer base) and creating an internal solution (expanding the brand through a logical merchandise extension). It was also a great example of overcoming resistance through tenacity and hard work and an example of patience overcoming force. It was a case of successful experimentation in something new that was well worth the effort, risk, and expense.

The lesson? Sometimes it helps to "go with the flow" and to appreciate that you control your own destiny. It's a lot easier when you have a little wind in your sails. That wind can be in the form of practicing presence, listening, yoga, or meditation. These are also tools that will help you implement the rest of the ideas in this book.

8

Life Is a Continuum of Beginnings, Middles, and Ends

THROUGHOUT OUR LIVES, IN VARIOUS ways, we are told to, "Stay calm and stick to your knitting." The previous chapter showed the importance of this advice at Men's Wearhouse: playing to our strengths was the difference between the failure in selling women's clothing and the runaway success of tuxedo rentals. But there is such a thing as too calm and too much sameness. Experimentation and every once in awhile reaching just outside the comfort zone are also important.

How, then, do you stay calm, stick to your knitting, and also experiment? The key is to understand that life is a continuum of beginnings, middles, and ends. The definition of continuum speaks to the thought that there is a link and a seamless transition between events. Nothing stays the same. You can calmly experiment. You can stick to your knitting while at the same time pushing yourself to explore the unknown. Nothing is static—and certainly this includes your own life.

In order to understand and appreciate that life is a continuum, take the long view and get some perspective. Think way back to what seemed like a very big problem in your life—maybe you were in the sixth grade and were worried that Sally or Sam didn't like you. In time, you managed to get through the crisis, and Sally/Sam is just a memory (pleasant or not). Think back to a more recent problem, one that in retrospect made the Sally/Sam issue insignificant. Perhaps it was choosing courses in college, or choosing your first job. Again, at the time it might have seemed monumental, but with the benefit of perspective, it's no longer that big of a deal. These examples are all part of your own continuum, just like any other learning experience that has occurred in your life.

The way our school systems are structured, we get trained to believe that life is linear. Things happen in a set order, starting at a very early age. You go to school and proceed from first through twelfth grade. After that, you might go to college or you might get a job. Either way, the next linear step is to find work, and perhaps find a partner. While that part of your life might in fact roll out that way, it's probably the last time that your life will be truly linear. The rest of life is far from it, but your mind and nervous systems have been trained otherwise—since the first grade.

Soon after you enter the workplace, your world becomes clearly separated. You have a work life, a home life, and a life that can best be described as your inner world—the part that deals with your personal development, if you so choose. It is then that you can better witness the continuum of your own life. Your nature wants you to treat all three of these the same—moving in the same linear fashion. But it's at this point that you have to extricate yourself from your linear existence and experience. If you don't, there is less potential for change, for growth, for effective problem-solving, and for rational decision making. This chapter will help sort out the continuum and give you the tools to deal with change and to solve problems.

A New Beginning:
From One Continuum to Another

Perhaps the idea of life as a continuum came to me later in life than it might for others. I did, after all, have a very long career with the same company. Yes, my job titles and responsibilities changed dramatically over twenty-nine years, just as Men's Wearhouse changed dramatically over those same years. But it was, by today's standards, an extraordinarily long career.

In a sense, even my decision to retire was a continuum, albeit a much shorter one than my career. At some point, I no longer saw myself working at Men's Wearhouse. And I saw that the best thing for my *self* was to start thinking about something else to do with my life. By then, the individual accomplishments had become part of the collective soup, and the line between my thoughts and contributions and those of others had faded away for me. I needed and wanted to do something else with my life. Off and on for several years before I made the actual decision, I'd spoken about retiring—mostly to myself. Initially, I was sure that I needed to devise a post-Men's Wearhouse plan while I was still working, so that I would feel less lost when the time finally came. Then it occurred to me: I wouldn't be doing the company or myself any favors by musing about being elsewhere *while* I was still at Men's Wearhouse, so I stopped thinking about it. I trusted that I'd know when the time to retire was at hand—or at least near.

In July of 2001, I had a clear sense that it was at hand. Facing retirement head-on was on my to-do list, as well as a long overdue conversation that I needed to have with a once-close friend, with whom I had lost contact over the years. On my way to the office one day, I decided to just go ahead and have that conversation. It was far less difficult than I had imagined it was going to be. On the contrary—it was great. With one to-do down and another to go, when I arrived at work, I proceeded to George's office, sat down with him, and told him that I was ready to retire. No doubt my experiences with yoga and meditation helped me to sense that this to-do list had to be shortened and gave me the perspective to know what to say, how to say it, hold my truth, and be calm all at the same time.

George and I had a warm, truly genuine conversation about what all these years had been like for each of us and for both of us. "So when are you thinking you want to do this?" George asked. My best guess was sometime between two days and two years, and I told him so. George was amenable to it, although he asked that it not be two days.

In November of 2001, I went to a retreat in the middle of the Arizona desert to try to sort many things out. I had been battling with my usual demons—mostly around fear—fear of relationships, fear of failure, fear of not knowing "what was next." Against the backdrop of the events of September 11th, the importance of making the best use of life called for attention. The retreat was recommended by a psychologist I trusted and deeply respected. So I went, with no expectations and a fair amount of trepidation.

One week into the ten-day retreat, while at lunch with three other people and discussing something not even closely connected to me or to my future retirement, a little voice whispered in my left ear, "You can't get out of there soon enough." There was no doubt about it—after a week of no TV, radio, phones, faxes, or newspapers, after literally being taken apart and put back together psychologically, and after intense meditation, that little voice was *very, very clear.* And that was it. I retired in January of the following year. I relied on my intuition to guide me to a decision I had wrestled with in another part of my being for a long time. The little, but very loud, voice didn't hurt, either. The voice was, for me, an amazing example how tuned in one can get when one is very quiet on many levels. And through this process, I saw very clearly how the end of one continuum is connected to the beginning of the next.

Living with Change

One of the big differences between the Boomer generation and that of their children is the career path. Boomers have tended to stay at the same job for most of, if not all of, their entire careers. At the least, they have stayed within the same industry. Now it is a given that those starting out will work at several different jobs over the course of their work career, and it's more than likely that they will change industries as well. Many will change fields entirely. As we've often heard, this generation needs the learning skills to prepare them for jobs that don't even exist yet. All of these changes make for a shift in reality that's important to understand: to cope with the job changes of the future, you're going to have to be comfortable with both the concept of change and the *practice* of change.

> *Be comfortable with both the concept of change and the practice of change.*

Change is a constant reminder that you are alive. The world we inhabit is always changing—more rapidly than ever. Indeed, change is inevitable and an absolute necessity for the survival of our species and our planet. Therefore, it is in your best interest to get comfortable with change and to be able to do it quickly, seamlessly, and in a way that best suits you. How do you deal with change? You can change that too: like so much else in life, it's a process and something to continually work on and refine.

The continuum of your life varies by situation. For example, at any one moment you can be at the beginning of personal transformation, in the middle of considering a big job change, or at the end of a relationship. In a certain sense, they're all separate and have to be treated as such in order to deal with them. But at the same time, and in a more important way, they're all part of a thematic ribbon—your personal development and the reminder that change is constant.

LIFE WITHOUT A MANUAL

Life is a learning adventure. And that's a good thing, for most of the really important parts of life aren't taught in any formal sense.

You learn by learning how to learn—by experiencing, by making mistakes, and by succeeding. You also learn by observing others—by seeing others make their own mistakes, and by seeing others succeed. As always, keep your eyes, mind, and heart open. The rest of this section presents a few areas to watch and to appreciate about your life and others' lives.

Life Is a Privilege. Regardless of your personal beliefs as to how mankind came into existence, one way or another life itself is a miracle—and a gift. You can use your gift of life any way you wish. You can choose to take it for granted, ride a wave of indifference, and hope for the best. Although that is a choice, it's probably not the best one. Another choice is to take the gift and "pay it forward" by leveraging your intelligence, insight, and experience into an opportunity for self-improvement and the improvement of others.

Life Comes with Responsibilities. First, you have to take responsibility for yourself. Then you have to reach outside yourself to help improve the lives of others and to leave the world in a little better shape than it was when you entered it.

Life Is a Challenge. Every day offers new challenges. Your life and these challenges require that you show up every day, ready to engage with the challenges.

Life Is Not Static. What is true and meaningful today might not be tomorrow. Life is knowing where you are in each and every moment (also known as being present).

Life Is a Process. Life is not a destination. There is no "there" there. Everything is all here—now.

Recognizing Fear and Overcoming It

Why do people resist change? First, it's human nature, especially when the change does not involve some immediate benefit. We all get rooted (and rutted) in who we are and what we do, and when our comfortable ways get threatened, our first reaction is to balk. When someone *else* comes along with an idea for doing something differently, our first reaction is usually, "Why? I've been doing it this way for …" In a situation where change is required, people involved will usually demand a reason for it. By nature, people prefer stability—and change represents a loss of stability. It has been said that there are only two things that are certain in life: death and taxes. I'd add one more thing—*change.*

The second reason for resisting change is fear. Fear is a natural reaction to change, but in the long run, it is not the reaction that serves us best. Pay attention to your fears; they hold enormous potential lessons. What kind of fear do most of us experience? Here's a sampling.

Fear of the Unknown. Nothing is easier to comprehend or live with than what you already know—even sometimes when what you know you *also* know isn't in your best interest. Fear can control us, or we can control it. Instead of letting the word *fear* have control, think of it as simply standing for, "False Evidence Appearing Real." If you can train your mind to *expect* the unexpected, you can let go of fear.

Stepping out into that place where you have less comfort and fewer expectations may seem frightening, but on another level, it is also fascinating. Forget the false evidence and go with the fascination.

Fear of Making Mistakes. No one *wants* to make a mistake. Mistakes can be embarrassing or induce feelings of guilt. But we are human, and we *all* make mistakes. Lots of them.

Fear of Guilt. Guilt is another ally of ego. The ego wants you to feel shame and blame for every mistake—big or little—that happens in your life. If you assume that on a moment-to-moment basis you are doing your best, you can stop guilt in its tracks. Relinquish guilt—you created it, you can destroy it.

Fear of Loss. Usually people fear losing something of importance or value, like money, friendships, freedom, or security. Also, people fear losing something they don't yet have or something they might really want to have. Instead of fearing loss, look forward to what you might *gain* by making any change.

Fear of Criticism. If you're being asked to change something, try not to assume it's because what is current is *wrong*. Try looking at it as *different*, instead of wrong—thus eliminating the voice of judgment. Stop criticizing yourself and others. When you criticize, you set up a hierarchy of "better than and worse than." The antidote for criticism is acceptance. Accept your own fallibility and the fallibility of others. When you forgive yourself, you set yourself on a path to learn to forgive others.

When you experience fear, instead of retreating, keep this in mind: fear is your soul's way of telling you that there is a great learning experience in front of you. If you have the voices of fear, worry, and doubt swimming around in your head, how are you doing to tame those voices? First, learn to accept that they are there. Second, remember that *you're* in charge—not the voices. Third, think about the fact that fear, worry, and doubt can be great motivators. Their purpose is to call upon your inner reserves and resources to experiment—to go outside your own box.

Resistance is one more visitation on your soul by your ego. Resistance is the ego's way of defending an opposite point of view. The ego doesn't like change and will do all that it can to keep you mired in your current situation, regardless of whether it's working for you. Pay attention to resistance. Resistance is also your body being stubborn. When you feel resistance, your body and your mind might be at odds with what you *think* you want or need to do. The body usually wins and says, "No" and you resist. Try letting the mind win once in awhile. Instead of thinking, try feeling—what feels good or right in the particular situation?

Practicing Patience; Finding Flexibility

As a society, we have been trained to expect instant gratification in the form of rewards or acknowledgment. Consequently, we give up easily to frustration when things don't happen the way we want or when we want them to. It's another aspect of the misadvertisement of life. Your life is not a sixty-minute television drama, where all loose ends miraculously get tied up at the end of the hour. The reality is this: just because the world moves fast doesn't mean that *you* always have to move fast with it. And the rewards or results that you might get are not necessarily on your timeline.

Patience is the ability to sit and wait for the outcome that *you* desire—in your own time and without becoming frantic. Patience is the same as trust; we are patient to the degree that we perceive that everything is in its right time, its right place, and moving in the right direction. Everything in your life is not going to fall into place immediately or perfectly—so watching, listening, staying calm and patient, and making alterations will help you to stay on course.

In the practice of yoga, you can often experience physical resistance. Some days your body is not as pliable as others. On those days, you learn to first back off a little and keep breathing, as a way to find out whether the resistance is coming from your mind or your body.

While on the surface yoga is all about physical flexibility, at its core, yoga also teaches flexibility in life. By breathing and being present, you can train yourself to take life as it comes at you, but at your own speed and with the willingness and capability to make adjustments when necessary. Emotional and mental flexibility—the ability to be able to quickly choose from different options in the face of changing conditions—is the hallmark of a mature nervous system and the hallmark of a mature human being. To be able to, at any moment, abandon all fear, all predisposed notions, and all sense of safety can allow you to be truly free. But it takes courage.

Being emotionally and mentally flexible means knowing that you don't know everything, and realizing that there is more knowledge in front of you than inside you. You don't know what the other person knows. There's a lot to learn by just listening.

Embracing Change

If life is change and resistance to it, how do we get through? Here are two ideas to help you get comfortable with change and be able to take it in with an open heart and an open mind.

LEARN TO ACCEPT CHANGE

Take a deep breath, smile, and know that like it or not—for that matter, accept it or not—change is all around us. You are far from alone in this. It's part of the fabric of our society. Take a look at the things that have changed in your life whether you wanted them to or not. The most obvious one is that you have gotten older. Be more open to the fact that there is nothing you can do to prevent a lot of the other changes in your life. Realizing that change is a fundamental part of your life will make accepting change less scary and stressful.

Start with small changes. There's change, and there's *CHANGE*. It's like the difference between decorating your apartment and moving to another city. Think small before you think big. Try the following everyday, stress-free changes for a while, and you might then find dealing with the bigger changes a little easier:

- Change some of the music you listen to.
- Change some of the websites that you frequent.
- Change your morning routine.
- Change a few items in your wardrobe.

By *doing* things a little differently, you will then be able to *experience* things differently and discover new ways to think, to see, and to allow change to begin to happen. While the above might seem like insignificant changes, once you train your mind to get comfortable with them, you'll notice that you can get comfortable with some slightly bigger changes. Go easy—it's a process, but the more that you do it, the better you'll get at it. Understand that there is knowledge sitting in all corners—often even the least likely ones. The key is to be open to the idea and to listen—not just to me in this book, but to the next wild hair and the next idea. Just because an idea or a thought doesn't conform to your picture of the world doesn't mean it's not valid.

After you've taken the small changes, before you know it, one day you'll actually find yourself *changing your mind*. Yes, it's amazing, but it will happen. You'll find yourself on one side of an issue, and the next thing you know—bam! You're on the other side. You're actually looking at all sides of an issue instead of digging in your heels on your position. It's an invigorating and exciting process. Push yourself by starting with the small changes. Try to experience at least one thing as new every day.

> *Just because an idea or a thought doesn't conform to your picture of the world doesn't mean it's not valid.*

Change Your Words; Change Your Outlook

As the poet Derek Walcott wrote (in "Codicil"), "To change your language you must change your life." How about turning that around: to change your life, change your words. I've already suggested that you delete some phrases and words from your everyday speech. Now I suggest adding some in. **Stop!** Think about the phrases "up until now," and "aside from that." If you can train yourself to say them any time a new idea or thought comes into your mind, or any time you are presented a new thought or idea by someone else, you'll automatically be more open.

How often do you come to a "new" situation with your "old" thought paradigm? "Up until now" is your reminder that every situation, although it may be similar to another one, is inherently different. "Aside from that" is your reminder that ideas are big things. Although you might disagree with a *part* of someone else's idea, if you don't allow yourself to get attached to that part, you can then move into the space where you can embrace the entire thought that someone else has. By doing this, you can learn to embody change. And you can learn to *create* change, by transcending your past and by creating a new and unfettered slate for your present and future.

Here are two other words to consider: "I wonder." Think about sending an "I wonder" out to the universe as a way to come up with a way to deal with change, and as a way to also come up with a new idea or, for that matter, to solve a problem. Picture the situation or problem and say, even just to yourself, "I wonder." You can make the "I wonder" be "I wonder how am I going to be with the change?" or "I wonder, what would a solution look like?" Sending an "I wonder" to the universe is essentially the first step in visualizing something entirely new.

Think of the old expression, "I'll believe it when I see it." There are circumstances when this phrase and the reporter's adage to "Believe half of what you see and none of what you hear" may be justified, but not when you're looking for ways to embody change or arrive at solutions to problems. In those cases, what about instead of thinking that you'll believe it when you see it, start thinking that you'll *see it* when you *believe it.*

Wait! There's one more way to change your words to change your outlook. It's actually more of a question—one that my father used to ask me. When you find yourself struggling or resisting change, ask yourself: "What's the worst that can happen?" Chances are that even the worst scenario is not that bad. And couldn't the reward be greater than the struggle or the resistance?

Lesson Learned:
Look Both Ways—and Listen

I started this chapter describing my decision to retire. There's another piece to it. Roughly a month before I retired, I met a woman who was about my age (and therefore also a Boomer), who had retired five years earlier. I really wanted to know what to expect, and although I was prepared for anything, I also knew I wasn't prepared for *everything.* Her comment to me was: "For the first three years or so, you're going to feel like you're walking around in the desert." I really didn't get what she meant until I actually lived through it. And she was right. Finding a new beginning takes time and effort, no matter what your experience level.

In a certain way, that time reminded me of an old black-and-white photograph that was taken of me at the Men's Wearhouse store one (of one), circa 1973. The photo encapsulated the beginning of a new continuum in my life way back when. In it I have hair on top of my head instead of my face, and I'm wearing a bow tie and a very busy nylon shirt. I'm standing next to a clunky old cash register with a rather dazed look on my face, not looking at the camera—or at anything in particular, for that matter. In the background is the store—vinyl asbestos tile floor, colored flags hanging off of a maze of steel bars, and signs that shout: "Double Knit Sport Jackets $27.75," and "Men's Suits $44.75." A friend of mine who saw that picture once said, "Did you realize at the time that Men's Wearhouse was going to turn out the way that it did?" I thought it was a pretty funny question and answered, "Do I *look* like someone who did?" Of course I didn't know it then—how could I have? I wasn't seeing into the future; I was more concerned with making ends meet. But on some level, I did have an inkling, so a more accurate answer is yes—and no.

I was young and open to possibilities. I was aware enough to be a container of receptivity—to be open enough for ideas, change, criticism, and overall knowledge. I was able to live with an enormous amount of change—from moving halfway across the country, to encountering resistances at the ad agency, to experiencing a new work environment. I stayed flexible and patient. It was all a self-taught and self-managed process, one that paid great dividends not only then, but in the years to come.

I realized *something* at the time, and looking back over the time and the effort, I'm not at all surprised by the company's success. Over the years, it had little to do with my contribution or me, as more and more had to do with the legacy created by the next generation of leaders. I *am* surprised at how so many other people—bankers, vendors, the soothsayers on Wall Street, and even some of our own employees—were surprised. And therein lies an important lesson. The lesson is to listen and pay attention, beginning with yourself. Had I listened to others' doubts and the kernels of self-doubt inside my own head, would I have prevailed? Probably not. You just never know. But in my case, listening to my stronger inner voice was certainly worth the risk.

Looking back, I'd like to say I paid full attention and by doing so, made my transition to retirement easier. But I was well used to being busy and, for the first few weeks after I retired, I got very busy right away. Soon enough, I found myself mad because I felt like my time—my precious time—was being eaten up by too many people asking for too many things of me. Then I realized that since *I* had contacted *them,* the person I needed to be mad at was myself. After calming down and meditating, I was able to realize that I was the one who was in control. So I redirected my efforts on getting involved in projects that fell into three categories and three categories only: they had to be fun, they had to be interesting, and they had to result in "greater good" somewhere along the line.

Having made those decisions and taken back the control, I remembered more of the uncertainty of the early days at Men's Wearhouse. Back when my continuum at the company had barely begun to play out, and the success of the company was nowhere near a sure thing, was it all luck? With the benefit of hindsight, I long ago came to realize that my success had nothing to do with luck. It had to do with the design for my own life—a design that changed over time.

9

Designing Your Luck;
Finding Your Place

LUCK DOESN'T JUST HAPPEN. THE saying, "The harder I work, the luckier I get" has been attributed to, among others, movie mogul Samuel Goldwyn, professional golfer Gary Player, and real estate developer Donald Trump, three very successful people who designed their own luck through hard work and persistence and with clear and definite goals for their lives. At some point, they realized that if they wanted to attain those goals, it was only going to be one way— through hard work. Ask any collection of successful people how they got to where they are, and you're bound to get the same answer—hard work. And you'll also probably find that their success had absolutely nothing to do with luck.

Luck by Design

My journey on the path to my "luck" began early, with a series of decisions, each of which led to another series of events unfolding.

After moving from Hazleton to Houston, I wound up on the steps of Men's Wearhouse. A short detour to my "dream" job at an advertising agency convinced me that the reality of that dream was far less than what I had expected. I then made a fundamental decision about where I wanted to be (Men's Wearhouse) and began to design my goals more consciously. I took risks, and I worked hard. I worked *very* hard. I succeeded—with a lot of help. And I failed—sometimes by myself, sometimes with a lot of help as well. When I failed, I recovered, kept getting up, and kept showing up. I was with Men's Wearhouse as it rose from a single store with a hand-painted wooden sign to a nationally known business with over five hundred stores. I retired from the company at the absolute perfect time for me and for what I wanted to do with the design for the rest of my life.

> *You're going to have to create your luck through your own hard work and design.*

The lesson? I created my luck—by design. And if I did it, *you* can do it.

If you want a rich, meaningful, and successful life for yourself, you're going to have to create your luck through your own hard work and design. This book has been dedicated to showing you how to do that, step by step. In this last chapter, I leave you with a few thoughts to help you piece it all together. The thoughts are not dissimilar to those back in the first chapter. Now, with the benefit of the knowledge you've gained in reading this far, you can better design your own luck and gain control of your life.

THE RESPONSIBILITY IS YOURS

If you haven't figured it out already, know the following: you are responsible for your own life and for what happens in your own life.

Yes, there is always the unexpected, both good and bad, but for the day-to-day events that occur, every bit of it is your responsibility and under your control. How do you keep things under your control?

First, make sure that you always have the ability to choose. You attain this by deciding whether you're going to be reactive or responsive. Choosing to be reactive is akin to saying, "Whatever happens, happens." Being responsive means that you take control over what happens and take the initiative to change the circumstances around things that might not be working for you. Choose to be responsive.

The second way to keep things under your control is to stay present, as described in chapter 3, "Everything Counts." Simply put, you can't let the outside world or any person around you tell you how you should think, feel, or act. Learn to trust your own intuition. It's your life and your design; own it.

Finally, dispel the notion that if left alone, problems will solve themselves. In fact, it's quite the contrary—generally problems that are left alone feed on themselves and become larger and less fixable. If things down the road are going to be better, *you* are going to have to make them better by the decisions and actions that you make *today*. There is no promise from any otherworldly source that you are being looked after or taken care of. Your life is one big experiment with many twists and turns, but certainly with no promises. Staying in control of your life means dealing with problems as they come up— as uncomfortable as that might be.

The best that you can do day to day is to keep showing up and learn to ride with everything, especially the rough spots, knowing and reminding yourself that you'll be just fine, even though there are no guarantees. That's a lot for one sentence, but trusting that it's the best path to follow *is* a great place to start. The lessons you've already read in this book should help clarify the idea as well.

TAKING THE RESPONSIBILITY

If the responsibility is yours, how are you going to *take* that responsibility? The process begins with creating goals and actions for yourself. You can begin that process by creating your own "Life Design." Perhaps you've read a book or an article that has suggested a similar idea—maybe by creating a personal mission statement, or a list of goals—and perhaps you have decided not to do it, because you thought the idea was silly or too time consuming. It's neither. Establishing your own Life Design is an example of *action*, as opposed to *intention*. We all have ideas about what we'd like to do with our lives, but unless you commit those ideas to words, they will be just a lot of random thoughts, generally resulting in little or no action.

At some point in life, we all can feel stuck, adrift, or have the nagging feeling that "there must be more to life than this." If you truly want to begin to design your own luck, creating your Life Design is a great start. Before you begin, here are three recommendations:

1. Be specific. When thinking about where you'd like to be at some point in time (otherwise known as "there"), *define* "there." Too often people create goals that they really can't get their arms around. Examples would be, "I want to be

successful ... I want to be happy ... I want to retire at an early age ..." I suggest a much sturdier and grounded "there." What is *your* definition of success? What is *your* definition of happiness? What *age* is in your retirement plan? Creating a Life Design is more than creating goals; it's creating *reachable* and *sustainable* goals. How do you know what is reachable and sustainable? You start by really knowing yourself, not only your strengths, but your weaknesses as well. You continue by (once again) getting comfortable with the fact that the answers are in your hands.

2. Remember that this Life Design is for your eyes only. Be honest and open. This is your own exercise, for *your* benefit. Don't write as if someone else were going to see it or comment on it.

3. Understand that your Life Design is not permanent. It is subject to change at any moment—by you.

If you want to print out a template for working through the Life Design process, you'll find one on my website: www.richiegoldman.com. If you prefer your own form, you'll need six pieces of paper.

- At the top of the first sheet, write: "These are the principles and ideas that are really important to me." Over the course of a week or two, write down those thoughts, ideas, and phrases that come to mind. Read them over right before you go to sleep to help your subconscious work. Think about and affirm everything you think you are and who you would like to become. Don't hold back: remember that anything is possible *when you allow it to be possible.*

- On the second sheet, write a list of "things that I'd be willing to change about myself in order to attain my goals."

- On the third, write a list of "things that I will not compromise in order to attain my goals."

Divide the remaining three pages into three columns each (work, physical, spiritual). For each question, you'll be describing what you want to be doing for work, and where you'd like to be in your life—as relates to your physical and spiritual place.

- Label the fourth page as: "This is what I'd like to be doing in one year."

- Label the fifth page as: "This is what I'd like to be doing in five years."

- And label the sixth page as: "This is what I'd like to be doing in ten years."

Once you've created your Life Design worksheets, you will have taken a giant step in taking responsibility for yourself. The next step is to replace intention (your Life Design statement) with action (what you actually to do about it).

Keep your Life Design where you can refer to it often. Reflect upon what you've written, and refine it when necessary. It is a living and pliable document, the blueprint for your life, and will require modifications as your life unfolds.

Make a conscious effort to live by your Life Design—to lead an intentional, rather than accidental, life. Focusing on your Life Design will keep you moving toward designing your luck.

Pain Is Inevitable; Suffering Is Optional

In his moving book, *The Last Lecture*, Randy Pausch writes: "No matter how bad things are, you can always make them worse" (page 88). Pausch, who was diagnosed with terminal pancreatic cancer and given only months to live, decided to make the most out of the time he had left. He decided to make things better and created a legacy for his wife, his children, and the millions of lives he touched with his lecture at Carnegie Mellon (which has since been broadcast widely via television and the Internet) and book. Pausch's intellect, abiding optimism, and sense of fun all shine through, both in the lecture and the book, immortalizing his role as hero and mentor to many.

No matter who you are and no matter how you live your life, you can be guaranteed that you will, at some point in your life, experience the following:

- You are going to be anxious.
- You are going to have fear.
- You are going to experience doubt.
- You are going to squander an opportunity.
- You are going to have regret.
- You are going to have your heart broken.
- You are going to experience the death of a close friend or family member.
- You are going to be disappointed by someone close.
- You are going to disappoint someone close.

How you manage and how you conduct your life after these negative experiences is all about your recovery—how you get back up when you fall down. To begin with, you can turn these events into life-altering experiences by demonstrating:

- Honesty
- Integrity
- Courage
- Strength
- Resiliency
- Growth
- Humility

Life is a constant process of recovery. It is when you're in pain that you learn the most about yourself and the most about your survival, humility, and ability to get back up and put yourself together. When you don't recover, you get stuck. When you get stuck, you lose the chance in the moment to learn and to grow. You also lose the chance to take control your life. When you don't recover, you fall victim to the event and lose control. Worse still, the less that you can recover in that instance, the less that you'll be *able* to recover the next time you need to. As a consequence, your world will continue to get smaller and smaller. No matter what the pain or how deeply it cuts, at some point after the initial shock wears off, you are going to have to develop a plan for recovery.

How do you recover? When something doesn't go the way you plan, crying a lot, complaining, or pointing the finger elsewhere isn't going to help. Ultimately, you're going to have to pick yourself back up. Part of the design for your life is how you get back up, and whether you choose to suffer (to make things worse) or to recover (to try to make things better). There is no universal cure-all for life's negative experiences. Each one has to be dealt with in its own time and space. But what you have read in the earlier chapters is a great foundation for you. When you can take every low point in your life as a learning experience, you will have added one more step in your ability to create your own luck by design.

The most painful and yet the greatest learning experience for me was in my painful life transition, back in 1998 (described in chapter 7). And now, years later, when I look back on it, I'm able to thank the universe and thank myself for the opportunity to learn and grow.

Why Are You Here?

At first glance, this might seem like an odd place in the book to be bringing up such big questions as why we are here on this planet, in this time, and why we are here individually. The questions that then might arise are what are we going to do, what is each of us going to do, and what are *you* going to do?

You might be wondering, "Why didn't he bring this up earlier?" The answer? Without the foundation that the book has presented, you might not be thinking about this question at the level that you are now. Sure, over the years you might have asked yourself why are you here, but my hope is that now, with the context and content of this book, you're prepared to think about this question in a more meaningful way.

Once you've begun to create your luck by design, you then have to ask, "What am I going to do with my life and my newfound luck?" That question might *then* bring up the next question: "Why am I here?"

Personally, I doubt that I was put on this planet to clothe Baby Boomer men. But through the process of helping to build Men's Wearhouse, I learned a lot about myself and about others in terms of how we all work, think, and share a wide variety of life experiences. Having been a part of Men's Wearhouse, I began to get a peek at why I am here. During the same period of time, I also began a series of personal explorations, completely separate from the company. These included such diverse topics as "Renewal," a three-day course I took at the Houstonian Hotel in 1980; "Learning to Feel," a weekend seminar at the Esalen Institute in Big Sur, California, in 1994; several yoga retreats; and of course, the desert experience in 2001.

The next steps for me have been the creation of the idea of this book, then the actual writing of it—intention, then action. It's my message to the next generation—my little piece of the puzzle that I'll leave behind. I don't know where it will all lead next, and that's part of the wonder of my life at this point.

Each of us has our own specific "true calling," an answer to the question, "Why am I here?" We need to feel that we are doing something worthwhile, that we are making a positive contribution to the planet. Sadly, many of us feel stalled or on standby, and we tend to sabotage ourselves with self-doubt, fear, and insecurities. But know that you are here on this earth at this time for several reasons. Broadly put, you are here to discover why you are here and what your purpose is; to find and tap into your divine source; to improve the world around you; to take care of yourself; and to have fun in the process.

LIVE AND DISCOVER

You are here to live the incredible experience of life that you've been given. Life itself is the discovery of why you are here. We are all flawed creatures who need to experience life in all of its capacities— good and bad. We have to make mistakes and feel failure in order to appreciate the imperfect world we live in. How you choose to live that experience is one of the fundamental challenges of your life. There are no universal answers—what matters is that you find the ones that work for you.

> *There are no universal answers—what matters is that you find the ones that work for you.*

You are on your life journey to fulfill your own sacred contract. This contract is something you are born to connect with—it is your reason and purpose for being alive. It is the essence of who you are; it is part of the path you are meant to travel during your lifetime. Your journey to find your sacred contract is just that—a journey. It's all about process and all about journey.

You are here to discover your "divine source." As children, perhaps even as adults, we think (or hope) that there is some divine spirit watching over us, making sure that all of the evils of the world don't happen to us, making sure that wrongs are righted, and making sure that we become our best person. It's a comforting thought, though (at least so far) unproven. In the meantime, how about this for comfort: the "divine source" isn't "out there"—it's *inside of you*. It's that place within that you will find when you slow down and get really quiet and really present. It's the place where you remember the life lessons that you have learned through your successes and failures. Another place to find your divine source is when you are teaching others. It is in this moment that you can run your own "reality check." There is no better way to find out if you have learned a lesson than by trying to teach it to someone else. Perhaps the clearest examples of passing on the lesson are through being a mentor or a parent. The former was covered in chapter 6, and the latter is something I haven't discussed too much up until now.

I can vividly recall the wonderful days with my daughter Emily when she was a little one. She was full of wonder, discovery, and excitement. And I've had the great fortune to experience the light of a child all over again—twenty-seven years later in life—with my second daughter, Ava. Extraordinary as my children are, I believe that all children can exude a magnificent sense of awe about all that is around them—every day being an experiment in the wonderment of life.

If you're not a parent, or not planning to become a parent, you can experience the same awe by watching kids. They can be nieces or nephews, godchildren, or cousins, or they can be kids that you interact with in the process of being a volunteer. No matter what the way, find a way, and get involved with kids. Your experience in doing this could be life-altering, for both of you. Not convinced? *Stop!* Stop, just for a moment, and think about a child's eyes, the openness and innocence you can see there. Children are born innocent, loving, and trusting; their sense of self, the world, and others is barely forming. For most children, the world is a safe place, and they readily trust themselves and others. Assuming no crisis of upbringing, children start out trusting and untainted, able to believe anything, especially anything of a positive nature. As just one manifestation of this, consider the fact that children also believe in the unbelievable—Santa Claus, the Easter Bunny, the Tooth Fairy, and Garden Fairies.

Why do children believe? What is it that enables them to blindly accept? *Lack of conditioning.* In a child's world, *every day* is a new experience, and the world is filled with nonstop wonder and first-time experiences. There is little "always" and "never." Children's uncomplicated lives are filled with endless experimentation and joy.

Why don't adults believe? *Conditioning.* Adults have trouble having experiences that are really new, because every experience reminds them, in some way, of a previous experience. The result of that previous experience makes it almost impossible to accept the unbelievable. Adults have had experiences that chipped away at their trust and faith in themselves and others. How can you counteract that? Reconnect with your innocence, your inner light, by observing a child's unguarded serenity, self-awareness, and free spirit. A child's energy can teach us to let go, trust, and connect with ourselves completely in the moment.

> *Reconnect with your innocence, your inner light.*

LEAVE FOOTPRINTS

You are here to leave footprints. Do your best to leave a path of learning and love for others to follow. Those "others" *should* be the ones closest to you and *can* also be nameless others who might cross your path. In leaving these footprints, and having an impact, it is also important to remember that you are both significant and insignificant.

You Are Significant. Realize and accept that you make a difference, and what you do over the course of your life makes a difference. We all make some sort of contribution, whether big or small, intentional or inadvertent. Every action has some sort of reaction. So if you live consciously, you increase your opportunities to make a positive difference. In contrast, if you don't give a damn, don't create meaningful relationships, and destroy many things that cross your path, you'll make a difference, all right—just a negative one. The very fact that you're here is quite remarkable, and although we all take it for granted practically all of the time, it's important to take a deep breath every now and then, look up into a blue sky, and be appreciative.

You Are Also Insignificant. After you're done looking up at the sky, remember that the world doesn't revolve around you, your ideas, or anything else that you might be involved with. Don't get too caught up with yourself. You are one of billions. Make your mark as your way of thanking the great beyond for the fact that you're here—no more, no less.

You Have a Gift. Each of us has a gift for another—the gift of ourselves. I call that gift generativity. You are here to create generativity by expanding the awareness of other people. You work and you live to teach and to help create a better world, to take your own knowledge and experiences and share them with your peers and with the next generation. You won't live forever, so you must seek to build a better world that you can live in and leave behind a positive legacy for the few people you know and the many people you don't. And every time you give, you're contributing to the legacy you're leaving.

We *all* have the capacity to be generative in different ways—as parents, teachers, mentors, leaders, friends, neighbors, volunteers, and citizens. It's not only in our nature, but it's also incumbent on us to do so. Here are a few ideas:

- Do something kind for yourself. Loving-kindness begins with knowing how to love yourself.
- Do something kind for someone else.
- Be grateful.
- Smile—for no particular reason. (You may well brighten someone else's day. If nothing else, people will wonder what you're up to.)
- Do something—do anything—differently than how you normally do.
- Make some music. (Even if that only means singing at the top of your lungs in the shower or in your car.)
- Ask someone else's opinion. Listen to it.
- Change your point of view.
- Admit that you made a mistake.
- Give some money away—to a charity, a school, or a friend in need.
- Become a mentor.
- Volunteer. You can volunteer your time, your expertise, or just about anything that you know that someone else might not know or might need.

- Forgive someone.
- Buy a gift for someone for no particular reason.

There are limitless other ways to practice generativity. Just as in making changes, you may find it easier to start small, build the habits, and then increase your ways of giving.

Take Care of Yourself

You have to take care of yourself. Seriously. I have written a lot in this book about service to others, but the first and most important place for this kind of service is to yourself. *Talk to yourself.* Don't get the wrong idea here. I'm not suggesting that you mumble to yourself while wandering aimlessly in public. What I'm suggesting is that you talk to yourself every day—with patience and kindness.

Patience begins with how you treat yourself. If you can't speak to yourself with kindness, it's unlikely that you'll be able to be kind to others. Practice talking to yourself in a loving and kind way all of the time. Eventually, this voice of kindness and compassion will become second nature as you're talking to yourself and interacting with others, and you'll be better equipped to open yourself up to all of the wonderful possibilities of who you are and who you are meant to be.

Another way to take care of yourself is to *have fun.* Learn to smile, laugh, and just be silly. Used at the appropriate time, these practices—smiling, laughing, being silly—can deflate tension and remind you that you are human like nothing else. And you'll just *feel better* when you're having (and sharing) fun. Yes, it's important to take life seriously, but it's equally important to not take all of life seriously all of the time. Go out there and have a good time.

At the end of the day when you ask, "Why am I here?" there is no standard one-size-fits-all answer. It's really just about you, and for you to find out. But on the road to finding out—if you travel that road with a conscious mind, an open and kind heart, with presence and intention—you will find the deeper meaning in everything you do, and it will dramatically improve your own power to be the person you *want* to be, and the person you were *destined* to be. You will be able to experience a happier and more fulfilling life, and in turn be more relaxed with yourself and your surroundings. This will enable you to attain greater success in all of your endeavors, be they personal or professional. Your personal, inside happiness can mitigate a great deal of unhappiness that may cross your path. Your full-time job is to be the generator of being whole, healed, happy, and healthy. From this place, your contribution has the greatest potential. How do you find all of this? Through continuous introspection and through living an authentic and empathic life. You will find it through continuous internal dialogue. You will also find it by trial and error and through external dialogue with your friends, family, and co-workers. It might take a lifetime to find this, but the journey is what your life is all about, and it's the most important journey you will ever take.

Lesson Learned: Making a Difference

Have you thought about incorporating the practice of generativity into your life? I have another suggestion about generativity to expand on one I gave earlier in this chapter. This variation may seem a little more difficult than the others. Whenever you are asked to, give money to people on the street who ask for it. **Stop!** You may have to re-read that sentence: Whenever you are asked to, give money to people on the street who ask for it.

Does it seem like a radical idea to give money to people on the street who ask for it, whenever they ask? What is this recommendation doing here? How is giving money away part of a lesson learned? It has to do with being present. It has to do with having a sense and awareness of those around us. It has to do with giving back. "But they're just going to use the money to buy drugs and/or alcohol," you might say. Maybe yes, maybe no. The point is, *you don't know.* We share this planet with all people. We don't know what brought a homeless person to this point, nor do we really know where that person's next meal is coming from. It is not ours to tell. Try to not be judgmental. Try to the right thing, look that person in the eye, and give a dollar or two.

Helping the homeless one-on-one like this is gratifying, but on a small scale. The city of San Francisco has taken it one step further with the creation of Project Homeless Connect (PHC). It was founded on the premise that people working in City Hall could better serve the community if they got out from behind their desks, at least once in a while, to see what was *really* happening in the community. The brainchild of San Francisco's mayor, Gavin Newsom, and his Deputy Chief of Staff, Alex Tourk, PHC is a partnership of the public and private sectors. Its goal? To create positive change in dealing with the homeless—changes that the city government either can't implement or doesn't have the money to implement by itself. The event itself is held about every six weeks, generally at the Bill Graham Civic Auditorium. It is, in a sense, "one-stop shopping" for the "clients" (as opposed to "homeless people")—a place where they can come and get food, clothing, arrangements for shelter, as well as psychological assistance, eyewear, or assistance in finding relatives. It's whatever the "clients" want.

While the origins of PHC were inside of City Hall, it soon became a volunteer effort staffed by average citizens, professional people, and businesses, all trying to lend a hand. The board of PHC created the nonprofit organization to raise the money needed to sustain it. The board is made up of people like myself who go to various community leaders and businesses to raise money to support the infrastructure and to raise awareness of PHC in the Bay Area.

PHC has been a runaway success—so much so that the idea has been taken and used in over 150 communities across the United States, including Denver, Minneapolis, and New York, as well as in Australia, Canada, and Puerto Rico. It is a classic example of how people working together with the same goal can create something great, without letting ego or desire for credit get in the way, and how all great things begin with one visionary idea.

The world works in mysterious ways. People can, without extraordinary effort, help to change a sour lemon into refreshing lemonade. And sometimes, having fun, doing good, and creating generativity can all come in one package. This is what I've witnessed personally in PHC. The camaraderie of the volunteers—people of all ages and backgrounds—is amazing to see. They are doing work that is very gratifying to them personally, and at the same time, they're having fun together. Their clients—also people of all ages and backgrounds—may be receiving more respect and positive attention than they have had in weeks. They all—volunteers and clients, alike—have smiles on their faces and gratitude in their hearts. And at the end of the day, one can be nothing less than appreciative of one's place on earth.

Your gift of generativity begins with the exploration of your inner self—discovering who you are and then finding the parts of yourself that you want to share and leave with others. The embodiment of your gift might come from your more practical side; it might come from your dream side. And remember, if you don't try to live your dream, you'll never know if it's right or what positive effects it might have, for you and for the world.

RICHARD E. GOLDMAN

PS...

You are here. Here at the end of this book. Here in this moment. Here to take over your life. A few parting thoughts:

There is a difference between hope and faith. Abandon hope. Always have faith. First, have faith in yourself and your abilities. You have the power, the knowledge, and the fundamental ability to make anything happen. Find that place deep inside of yourself that you know is there. That part that you might have hidden for a long time—the part that might you fear because of its power. Now is the time to use it. You are about to venture out into a world that you inherited— make it better. Make it safer. Make it more loving and caring than anything that you ever might have imagined.

Have faith in other people as well. Don't succumb to the media's lowest common denominator of dumbness, meanness, and "gotcha" mentality. Rise above it and soar to your own greatness. Do you want to take back your life? Take it back through fundamental kindness, fairness, and respect, one person at a time. Take it back by having faith that even the tallest buildings are built one brick at a time. Kindness, fairness, and respect are contagious. Spread them around. Do you want to take back your country? It's been said that the United States is the last best hope on earth. You are the last best hope for the United States. As I noted in the Open Letter at the beginning of this book, the problems that we all face in the world aren't the result of any one person. And they won't be solved by any one person. But maybe, just maybe as the result of your reading this book, a spark has been generated in you to go out there and make your best effort at resolving the problems.

We Boomer parents, who grew up with the Cold War, were taught to prepare for the worst—nuclear annihilation. We did so by building fallout shelters. Your worst is certainly scary as well, but here's a thought: instead of preparing for the worst, why not prepare for possibilities? Prepare for the *best case*, because to a great extent, you *can* control it.

You already have everything you need to make it happen.

Go MAKE SOME LUCK HAPPEN!

At the end of most yoga classes, after the final savasana (a resting pose), there is often a moment of thought or prayer, and the instructor usually ends by gently bowing to the participants and saying, "Namaste." This is Sanskrit for, "I bow to the light that is you." It's a way of seeing and acknowledging the special qualities that each of us has. It is a way to appreciate and embrace the abundant potential and endless possibilities in every person whose path you cross—your partner, spouse, child, parent, co-worker, boss, customer, and above all, yourself.

This is the end of *this* journey for me. It is also the beginning of a new journey for me, as well as a new journey for you …

Namaste …

References

Cleary, Thomas, trans. *Zen Lessons: The Art of Leadership.* (Boston: Shambhala Publications, 1989).

Farhi, Donna. *Yoga Mind, Body, & Spirit.* (New York: Henry Holt and Company, LLC, 2000).

Gafni, Marc. *Soul Prints: Your Path to Fulfillment.* (New York: Fireside, a division of Simon & Schuster, 2002).

Kabat-Zinn, Jon. *Wherever You Go, There You Are: Mindfulness Meditation in Everyday Life.* (New York: Hyperion, 1994).

Keen, Andrew. *The Cult of the Amateur: How Today's Internet Is Killing Our Culture.* (New York: Doubleday, a division of Random House, 2007).

Kundera, Milan. *Slowness.* (New York: HarperCollins, 1996).

Kundtz, David. *Stopping.* (Berkeley: Conari Press, 1998).

MacKenzie, Gordon. *Orbiting the Giant Hairball: A Corporate Fool's Guide to Surviving with Grace.* (New York: Viking Penguin, 1998).

Pausch, Randy. *The Last Lecture.* With Jeffrey Zaslow. (New York: Hyperion, 2008).

Peters, Tom, and Robert Waterman. *In Search of Excellence: Lessons from America's Best-Run Companies.* (New York: Warner, 1982).

Strand, Clark. *The Wooden Bowl: Simple Meditation for Everyday Life.* (New York: Hyperion, 1998).

von Oech, Roger. *A Whack on the Side of the Head: How You Can Be More Creative.* 25th Anniversary Edition, revised and updated. (New York: Business Plus, 2008).

Acknowledgments

I HAVE TAKEN ON MANY partners in the process of writing this book and living my life. I want and need to thank them, and at the risk of showing favoritism, I'll do so alphabetically. Granted, my alphabetization—by first name—is unusual. And it feels right to me, for it underscores my thanks to my father and my wife—first and last.

Aaron Goldman, my father. For giving me the wings to fly and instilling in me the fundamental and vital sense of fairness.

Advisory Board. For your insight, input, and interest. You've made this a much better book.

Charlie Bresler. A great leader and a great friend.

Cheryl Malakoff. Who pulled me out of more spiritual holes than I could ever begin to articulate, and who was my "ghost editor." A true joy and wonder.

Dan Goldman, my brother. Some great stories of our early years didn't make it into this book, but it was fun writing them and thinking about our childhood together.

Emily Goldman, my daughter. For having the guts to call this thing a book long before I did and setting me straight about what it was about. It's great to learn from your kids.

Eric Lane. Another terrific leader and friend, Eric inherited one of my jobs (General Merchandise Manager) and greatly improved on my efforts.

George Zimmer. A very important person in my life.

Ivan Cury. A patient teacher of the "biz" of making commercials. The movie rights for this book are yours.

Janet Hunter, my editor. You "got it" and me right away. You kept me focused, yet gave me enough rope to creatively swing. It's been a pleasure and an honor to work with you.

Jayme Maxwell. Jayme inherited my job as the head of Marketing and Advertising and did it better. Your style, tenacity, and sense for simply what is right have meant a lot to me.

Jordan Morganstein. An inspiration, a teacher, and a believer in Men's Wearhouse from the early years. Also one of the most honest people I've ever met. I miss you and think of you often.

Kim Grubbs. Thank you for just listening and pushing me when I needed it.

Kristen Feenstra. You showed up when I needed you most and gave me an appreciation for yoga that I never would have discovered otherwise.

Lonnie Hanzon. Amazing artist, incredible inspiration, but more than anything else, a wonderful friend.

Mary Zubrow, my sister. Not only are you my sister, but you are also my very good friend. How great is that?

Men's Wearhouse, my work family. While you aren't all mentioned by name, your spirit and your contributions have made the company successful, and they have made my writing this possible—and, I trust, worthwhile.

Morgan-James, my publisher. Everyone at Morgan-James. And a special thanks to David Hancock, for having faith in this book while it was barely an outline.

Reba Goldman, my mother. I don't know how you managed to raise the three of us and keep your sanity, but you did, and we all think of you often.

Samuel Goldman, my grandfather. I hardly knew you, but somehow I did, and your voice and spirit are part of my soul.

Traci Mitchell Goldman, my wife. For your unconditional love and support, and for knowing when to leave me alone and when not to. I've learned a lot from you by just observing.

About the Author

Born in Hazleton, Pennsylvania, Richie Goldman graduated from Rutgers University in 1972 with a BA in English. The following year, he moved to Houston, Texas, with his degree, his car, a bit of advertising experience, and $300 in hand. After a series of "lucky" decisions, he met George Zimmer and went on to help create Men's Wearhouse, one of the largest men's apparel retail companies in North America. While at Men's Wearhouse, Goldman was the general merchandise manager for many years and was responsible for the marketing and advertising of all brands. In 1992, Men's Wearhouse went public (NYSE: MW). During his tenure, Forbes Magazine recognized Men's Wearhouse as one of the "100 Best Companies to Work For" and Men's Wearhouse was named "Retailer of the Decade" by MR Magazine, the leading national trade magazine for menswear retailing.

Since his retirement from Men's Wearhouse in 2002, Goldman has shared his managing, marketing, and professional expertise in numerous ventures, consulting with retailers and manufacturers across the country. He is a founding Board Member of San Francisco Connect, the innovative public-private effort to eliminate/control homelessness in San Francisco (sfconnect.org), and is a former board member of The Jewish Community High School of San Francisco. He has been a board member, investor, and consultant to Benefit Magazine, a magazine dedicated to philanthropy in the greater Bay Area. He has also worked on the political campaigns of several candidates, most notably Gavin Newsom, both in 2003 and 2007. He was on the Board of Trustees at Mills College from 1999-2005, and is currently on the Board of Overseers for the Graduate School of International Business and Finance at Brandeis University. He is a founding member of the Milton S. Friedman Lecture Series at Rutgers University. He has spoken on Wall Street, to business groups, and to audiences in high schools and universities about his experiences at Men's Wearhouse, in business, and in life.

Luck by Design: Certain Success in an Uncertain World is Goldman's first book—and he is already at work on his next. Goldman and his wife, Traci, live in northern California with their daughter, Ava. Much to their delight, Goldman's older daughter, Emily, and her daughter, Zaia, live nearby.

Printed in the USA
CPSIA information can be obtained
at www.ICGtesting.com
JSHW012015140824
68134JS00025B/2430